YOUR JOURNEY TO SUCCESSFUL PARENTING

AGES 2–11

A STRESS-FREE GUIDE TO
EFFECTIVE BEHAVIOR CHANGE

ALEXANDRA J. ROGERS, PHD

First edition 2025.
Published by A Rogers Books LLC
Austin, TX
https://arogersbooks.com

Cover design by 100 Covers
Interior design and typesetting by Mayfly book design

Library of Congress Control Number 2025903067

ISBN (hardcover) 979-8-9916156-0-0
ISBN (paperback) 979-8-9916156-1-7
ISBN (ebook) 979-8-9916156-2-4

Dedication

This book is dedicated to parents who struggle to raise their children to be the best versions of themselves and to caretakers baffled by behaviors that don't make sense.

Contents

Part 3: Frequent Situations Encountered by Parents

Part 4: Concerning Situations That May Require Professional Intervention

Introduction

It was a career-defining moment for me. I was leading a therapy group of hyperactive boys between the ages of eight and ten. The six of us were crowded into a small office. This was my first children's group, and I didn't know what to expect. These boys taught me my first great lessons.

In the first session, one boy kicked another, causing a chain reaction of kicking. We moved from the couch and chairs to the floor.

The following week, there was another round of kicking, but this time, I saw who gave the first kick. We moved to the floor again, and I observed the boy who started it. The other four boys talked a lot, but the boy who gave the first kick did not participate. Because I was watching him, I smiled whenever he looked at me. He smiled back.

The kicking stopped. I assumed that the kicking was his way of making himself noticed.

One time, a boy came to the group very tense and upset. I asked if he wanted to sit on my lap until he calmed down. He nodded and sat on my lap, facing the other boys. I assumed he'd be embarrassed and that the other boys would make fun of him, but they all acted as if it was the most normal of sessions and continued talking.

We sat like this, rocking slowly, until I felt his body relax. Then I asked if he was OK with going back. He said yes and sat in his spot.

Another time, a colleague talked to me about one of the other boys in my group. His dad was deployed for six months, and the boy behaved horribly after his father left. The psychologist wanted to know if the boy needed to be medicated. Because this young man didn't show any behavior issues during the groups, I asked him how his mom was dealing with his dad's deployment. He said, "Not good." I asked if he misbehaved on purpose so that Dad had to return, and he said, "Yes." My last question was, "Did it work?" The boy said, "Yes." I told the fellow psychologist that he did not need medication.

This group experience occurred early in my career; the first lessons I gleaned were the most influential:

- People who can't express themselves verbally try other means of communication. No one likes to be overlooked or ignored.
- You can acknowledge someone with a smile so that they feel seen.
- You can help someone relax without using words and transfer your calm energy to them.
- Most behavior is purposeful. You need to figure out what the ultimate payoff is.

These were only a few of the lessons I learned from my patients.

I wasn't born knowing everything. There was confusion, curiosity, aha moments, and understanding.

This will be your experience as you read this book. I assume you bought it because you haven't found the key to unlock the behaviors in your children that you want to see more of. This book gives you the keys through examples, recommendations, and explanations of what works and why. Some examples will mirror your struggles with your children; others deal with situations you haven't encountered yet but may in the future.

There are many causes of misbehavior and lack of cooperation in children. Some children live in a world where they observe you and their peers and test what behaviors work. Others are so disruptive that it's hard for you to take them anywhere. You get flustered and frustrated trying to manage the behaviors while ignoring the disapproving stares of onlookers.

Some of you are baffled because your children have been perfect angels—until now. You've tried everything but haven't been able to turn things around. Perhaps your children have tested your patience and authority, and you're fed up, exhausted, and frustrated. Or your children have developmental issues, disabilities, and mental health problems, and you're trying to separate correctable behaviors from their struggles with the other issues.

All children and parents have personalities. The interplay between you and your children depends on your requests and expectations, which are based on your personality style, and your children's reactions to those requests and expectations, which are based on their temperament and internal experience. The challenge is to navigate through all these differences and pick the best intervention.

Personally and professionally, I like to keep things simple. In my writing, I seek to show the basic commonalities in what triggers behaviors and offer recommendations that work with most children.

I enjoyed working with children and parents throughout my thirty-two-year career as a clinical psychologist in California. Many of the problems that brought them to my office were similar. My work included psychological and neuropsychological testing, classroom observation, individual therapy, group therapy, and parent-child therapy. Over the years, I distilled some treatment recommendations that worked in most situations. These recommendations form the essence of this book.

In semiretirement, I have the time to reflect and write. Our world has changed, as have parents' and children's problems. I chose to write about kids ages two to eleven partly because some of the issues respond to the same interventions and partly because our kids grow up so fast that what used to be teen issues crop up earlier. If your children are young, you may want to keep this book for future reference.

Please think of this volume as a handbook. You can jump around and read the chapters in any order.

Part 1 provides the building blocks for examining issues and behaviors. It includes interventions for the discussed problems.

Part 2 focuses on interventions that encourage some behaviors and discourage others. It explains why some methods work and others fail.

Part 3 addresses challenging behaviors frequently encountered by parents. It explains the behaviors and offers ways to repair the situations.

Part 4 contains uncommon situations that may or may not be part of your struggle with your children or preteens.

This book is the first in the Your Journey to Successful Parenting series. I'm currently writing the other books:

- *Your Journey to Successful Parenting: Teens*
- *Your Journey to Successful Parenting: Autism and Hyperactivity*

PART 1

A New Way of Looking at Interactions Between Yourself and Your Child

ONE

The Magic of Attention

Kids are wonderful. They teach you about life, love, persistence, and exhaustion. You see your reflection in their actions as they copy you. Each day is a revelation as they try to maneuver you into doing something for them or act in startling ways. But above all, they want your love, admiration, and attention. Problems start when you stop paying attention because of work demands, the need for a break, or exhaustion.

You May Be Surprised That Many Misbehaviors Are Attempts to Get Attention

Your young ones depend on you for food, shelter, love, attention, and approval. If they can't get your approval and attention by doing good, they resort to anything that gets a reaction from you.

We are swamped every day, and when the kids are quiet, it is easy to overlook them. Ignored children frequently resort to misbehavior. Even punishment is better than being ignored.

The following are two examples of a child intentionally misbehaving for attention:

Example 1: You are in a Zoom meeting. Johnny appears in the doorway despite being told not to interrupt you. Silently, he shows you his bleeding leg. Johnny scratched off one of his scabs.

Example 2: You have friends over for dinner. The conversation is animated. You are having a great time until Sally begins eating like a dog.

Such behaviors take place when your kids feel overlooked.

Johnny does not mean to be self-harming. He's just learned that blood gets your attention. There's nothing wrong with Sally. She's three years old and cannot participate in adult conversation. Sally felt ignored, so she did something to get attention. You noticed!

Be proactive in stopping your children's attention-seeking behaviors.

Take Time During the Day to Show Love, Attention, and Admiration

Children need to know you love them. When your kids are young, smiling, caressing, hugging, and kissing are sufficient. If they are playing quietly in their room, you can look in on them and smile. These gestures let them know you love them and like having them around.

If you have preteens at home, you know that any show of affection invites a rebuff. However, if you stop trying to show them you love and admire them, they become upset and angry. They still need your love, even though they seem to be pulling away from you. With preteens, you can show love by admiring actions and achievements they are proud of.

You can deal with Johnny's situation, from the first example, by stopping by his room before you get on Zoom, chatting a little, looking at what he's doing, and showing interest and approval. Assure him you will check back with him after the Zoom meeting. When the meeting ends, go to Johnny and see what he's been doing or creating.

In Sally's situation in the second example, ignore the doglike behavior. When she stops, look her way and smile. Include her in the conversation to prevent inappropriate attempts to get attention. Tell the guests about Sally's latest accomplishments. Show off Sally's artwork or whatever else she may be proud of. Look her way during the adult conversation and smile multiple times.

Taking time out of your busy schedule to be with your children is another way to show them you love them and enjoy their company.

Use Phone Conversations to Let Your Children Know You're Proud of Them

Children are very interested in what you think of them. Therefore, when you mention their name on the phone, their ears prick up. Children who cannot hear you shouting at them to clean their room hear every word of a whispered telephone conversation about them.

Be very careful about what you say about your youngsters within their earshot. If you talk about Johnny's positive behaviors and accomplishments and skip the misbehaviors, he knows you appreciate and notice his good deeds. But if you talk about Johnny's misdeeds and forget the good, he gets the mistaken idea that you only notice the unwanted behaviors, and the misbehaviors spike.

Example of a Conversation About Your Youngster Within His Earshot

Johnny hit his little brother because he was bugging him. Later in the day, he shared a cookie with his brother. You get on the phone with a relative, lower your voice, and report the positive.

You: "Grandma, you'll never guess what Johnny did today! He shared his cookie with his brother without me asking him to!"

You skip the part about Johnny hitting his brother earlier in the day. The following day, Johnny didn't hit his brother. You get on the phone that evening and, in a lowered voice, tell a relative:

You: "I'm so proud of the boys, Aunt Emmy. They played nice all day. Not a single fight. They were loving brothers all day."

Remember, much of misbehavior is all about attention!

How to Get Your Child's Attention

At home, we tend to call out instructions to one another. We don't behave this way at work or with friends. Some family members interpret calling out instructions from another room in the house as a lack of love and respect and pretend they don't hear you. This includes children and adults.

Explain this to the whole family and encourage everyone to stop calling out instructions and requests from another room. Make the personal approach a family standard to prevent the ignoring behavior. If your children have developed a habit of ignoring you even when you are standing right next to them, then you must create a new habit. To create a new listening habit, repeat the following steps many times:

1. Approach your child and stand in front of them before you start speaking to make eye contact.
2. You can get your child to look at you by touching their arm or face and saying, "Look at me" or "Point your eyes at me."
3. Wait for eye contact before you make your request calmly and respectfully. "Can you please . . . ?"

If your child avoids eye contact, stop insisting on it. How do they let you know they are ready to listen? Do they turn in the direction of your voice? Do they begin rocking or stop rocking when they are listening? Do they tilt their heads? You can ask your children to touch your fingertips to let you know they are ready to listen. Keep your requests simple.

Your child is not the family dog. The dog is happy to come running when you call, but you never ask your dog to clean his room or do other unpleasant chores. It sounds basic, right? However, we often forget to address family members respectfully. Attention is important to all family members but is essential for children. You'll find parenting enjoyable and rewarding once you harness the power of attention.

You may point out that it's not so simple. There are other causes of misbehavior. You're right. For example, children who cannot express themselves become easily frustrated if you don't guess what they need or how they feel. This can lead to loud outbursts, smashing, scratching, or hitting.

We began with the basics, which are often overlooked and easy to repair. Please try the methods in this chapter. You'll be pleasantly surprised by the results.

Some misbehaviors may become entrenched and become habits and behavior patterns within families. The next step is learning how to break up long-standing, infuriating patterns.

TWO

Patterns and Habits

Most Behaviors Are Simply Patterns and Habits

You might read this heading and think, *Wait! What?*

Notice your behavior as you go through the day. Much of what you do follows a familiar pattern. You drag yourself out of bed in the morning, head to the kitchen for coffee, make breakfast, and then wake everyone up. You say the same things to your spouse, your kids, and the family pet.

There is a reason for the consistency. Your brain looks for sequences of behaviors and develops neural networks to handle chains of behaviors. It's all about efficiency. Your brain learns to create efficient networks to handle complex muscle and attention sequences.

For example, when you start playing soccer, your mind is focused on kicking the ball. Then, as you get good at kicking, you focus on kicking the ball into the goal. Eventually, all those actions feel automatic, and you can focus on where the other players are on the field. People call the automatic actions *muscle memory*—but the memory is not in the muscles. Your brain is directing all the activity.

Repetition of sequences of behaviors leads to the formation of habits.

Repetition Creates Habits

We all have our clusters of habits and patterns of behavior. Repetition of the same actions and verbalizations creates habits. You can develop good habits or bad habits. Your kids can also develop good or bad habits via their behavior patterns. For example, your son develops a habit of grabbing everyone's toys without asking first. Introducing him to a new sharing pattern can replace the toy-grabbing habit. Now you can stop worrying about your son becoming selfish.

What if your child writes sloppily, without spaces between words or punctuation at the end of sentences? If you allow the action to continue, a habit will be created. Their brain will learn to write poorly. Instead, intervene and have your child practice and rewrite everything. Your youngster will fume, but in the end, their brain will learn how to direct their muscles so that they can write neater. The brain learns by repetition.

You may point out that your child has dysgraphia (problems holding writing implements and forming letters that stay on the line). After a while, you notice that your child has developed a specific writing style. His style is the result of repetition. If teachers cannot read the writing, it needs to be improved.

Observe your child to ensure they develop the habits you want to encourage.

Interactions Can Become Habits and Patterns

Sometimes the interactions with loved ones are pleasant and make everyone feel good. Other times the conversations and activities make everyone feel bad, mad, or uncomfortable.

Have you noticed that some of your interactions with others have become a repeated pattern? You can tell you are in a habitual conversation when you find yourself saying something and knowing how the other person will respond. After this initial exchange, you know what you will say next and what they will say in response. The conversation feels as if you're participating in a weird play in which each of you repeats your rehearsed lines. You know the scene will end badly. Yet you repeat the conversation time and time again.

But you don't have to repeat your part. You can change the script.

The easiest way to break the unhealthy pattern is to avoid saying your line.

Stop talking.

Watch as the other person prompts you to speak your expected lines correctly. As you get better at identifying some of the patterns of interaction, you can plan how to change the script and regain control of the conversation.

Can you think of any unpleasant patterns of interaction with your child? If so, you can plan how to change them. I've included a couple of common scenarios next.

Electronics Example

You: "Jake, it's time to turn off the game and get ready for bed."

Jake: "Inaminute."

You: "Please turn off the game."

Jake: "Can I have five more minutes?"

You: "No. It's late."

Jake: "You used to give me a five-minute warning."

You: "Yes, when you were five years old." Now you are at Jake's doorway. "I need to get back to my work emails. Turn it off now!"

Recommendation

Set a daily schedule for turning off all electronics to create a habit. After a time, your interactions morph into the following:

You: "It's ten o'clock!"

Jake: Jake slams the controller and turns off the game.

Homework Example

> You: "June, it's time to start your homework."
> June: "I don't have any homework."
> You: "Let me see your planner."
> June: "I forgot it at school."
> You: "Your teacher says she gave an assignment."
> June: "I finished it at school."
> You: "Let me see it."
> June: "I already submitted it."
> You: "I want to see it. Get your computer out."

Recommendation

Explain that you want to see all the homework. Most homework assignments these days are electronic. If June turns in the completed assignment, the system shows it as accepted.

If there is a recurring problem of June failing to do or submit her homework, you can set up a behavior chart with points as an incentive. She gets the most points for completing an assignment correctly, half the points if the work needs to be redone, and zero points if she did nothing. Chapter 12 discusses behavior charts. It describes how to set them up and keep track of desired behaviors. Behavior charts work well for forceful and stubborn children. From the kids' perspective, they perform the desired behaviors to get the rewards, not because you asked them to.

After the behavior chart is in place, you can expect the following interaction:

> You: "June, show me all your homework. Let's see how many points you earn on your chart today."
> June: "I didn't finish all of it yet."
> You: "OK. When you're done, let me know, and I can look it over."

Why do Jake and June behave in such ways? Whom are they copying?

THREE

How Children Learn

Copying

Children learn by copying those around them. Your kids copy what you do and say. As toddlers, they become miniature caricatures of you. Children imitate characters on TV and the kids on the playground. Later in life, they use peers and teachers as models. You can use this process of copying to mold their behavior.

To teach new behaviors, model the actions you wish to see in your child. A fashion model models clothes. You model behaviors and verbalizations. If your child is behaving in a way that you don't recognize as your own, do the following:

- Ask yourself, "Does someone in our family behave in such a manner?"
- Ask your child, "Whom are you copying? Who does [name the behavior]?"

Sometimes the behaviors are very subtle and are part of a habitual pattern. I've included some examples next.

Phones at the Dinner Table

You sit down with your family for dinner. Your son and husband are busy on their phones as they eat. There is no conversation. If you try to say something, you feel ignored and overlooked. Your son is copying his dad. Dad uses the excuse that he has to answer emails.

Yelling to Request Help

You ask your husband to change a light bulb. He says OK but doesn't move. You get louder and request that he change it *now*. Some days later, your son asks for help with his homework while you're cooking dinner. You tell him, "Later. I'm in the middle of cooking." The boy shouts that he needs help *now*.

Parents as Models

When kids are small, Mom is their model for all the women in the world, and Dad is their model for all men. If Mom is disrespectful, disregards Dad's comments, and shows her disapproval of what Dad achieves, the daughter may grow up to think all men are no good. The son might believe he can never please Mom because she disapproves of men. The daughter can change her mind as she becomes introduced to other men, but she will harbor the suspicion that women are superior. The son may grow up believing he can't please any woman.

If Dad is disrespectful toward and dismissive of Mom, the son may grow up thinking women are not to be taken seriously and won't listen to Mom and other women. Because most teachers are women, he will be perceived as having behavior problems at school.

These examples illustrate your influence in forming your children's perceptions of the world. Check yourself as you speak around your kids. Teach by example. Provide a model for how you expect your children to act. You are forming their belief systems.

Shaping Behavior

Shaping behavior refers to teaching new skills in a way that encourages any effort toward the behavior you want them to learn. The reward is praise and encouragement. Use this method when your child struggles to learn a new skill.

Shaping Behavior to Encourage Early Walking

Your little Lee is learning to walk but doesn't like falling, so he hangs on to you or the furniture when he walks. You want him to hurry up and learn how to walk unassisted. Your back hurts from carrying him and from bending over so that he can hang on to your hand.

Recommendation

Watch your Lee while the TV plays his favorite show. Encourage him to walk along the coffee table as he is absorbed in the show. Occasionally, he might forget to hold on as he takes a step.

You: "Lee, you walked without holding on to the coffee table. Keep walking around the table. I will make a video for Daddy."
Keep your voice even. You don't want to spook him and cause a fall. Keep him walking around the coffee table and start filming. From time to time, he forgets to hang on.

You: Show him the video. "Look, Lee. You're walking without holding on. That was great. We have to show it to Daddy."

Lee: Lee looks pleased.

You: "See? You can do it."
Next, stand a foot away from Lee. Ensure that it's an open area so that he doesn't hit against something if he falls.

You: "Now I will stand here, and you come to me."

Lee: Lee hesitates.

You: "You can do it. Look, you did it before." Show him the video again. "I'll stand right here."
Stretch your hands just out of his reach so that all he has to do is take one step.

Lee: Lee makes the step.

You: "You did it. Let's do it again."
Again, stretch your hands out so that all he has to do is take one step.

Keep repeating the process, gradually increasing the number of steps. You want him to be successful, so make sure you don't go beyond his ability to balance.

Shaping Behavior to Get Rid of Fear of the Swimming Pool

Your little Lee loves water but is afraid to go into the pool. He watches the other kids having fun but refuses to go in. Encourage him to lie down on the concrete or tile by the wading pool and stick his hand in the water. Once he's comfortable splashing the water with his hand, ask him to sit on the edge of the wading pool and put his foot in the water. Next, have him splash with his feet to make the water go high. By now, he is having fun splashing. This is the time to ask him to sit on the lower step of the pool so that the water comes up to his chest. Give him a toy to play with.

You: "It's just like playing in the tub. Now you're just like the big kids."

Shaping is a great tool for parents, teachers, and coaches. Next, let's explore social learning based on copying social behavior.

Social Learning

Social learning is based on observing and copying the behavior and interactions of others in the community. You don't have control over what your child observes at school, in the community, and on the playground. There are many people to copy. Your child must identify who is friendly, approachable, popular, or mean. They must figure out who seems happy to play with whom. Whom can they imitate as they watch the kids in the yard? Sorting this out takes a lot of observation. Shy kids take several days to sit on the sidelines and observe. Children exposed to new social situations earlier in life have an easier time because they've done this before.

You can support social learning outside the home by taking your child to playgrounds or by inviting kids to your house. During these times, watch your child. Who catches their attention? Later, you can discuss the events.

Example of Social Learning Support

You invite some of Sue's friends to your house for a playdate. When the guests leave, the following exchange occurs:

You: "Did you have a good time with your friends?"

Sue: "Yes. When can we do it again?"

You: "Soon. Did you see how Kathleen behaved before her mother took her home?"

Sue: "She wouldn't let me have my doll back. Her mom told her she needed to share with me because I shared with her."

You: "Then what happened?"

Sue: "She threw the doll at me."

You: "How did it feel?"

Sue: "I was scared she broke my doll. I don't want her to be mad at me."

You: "Of course you don't. What happened then?"

Sue: "Kathleen's mom told her she wasn't playing nice, so they had to go home."

You: "I'm glad you're good at sharing. It makes playtime more fun."

Sue: "Can Kathleen come over again? I like her when she's not being mean."

You: "Of course. I'm sure Kathleen can learn to share."

Sometimes you have to undo some behaviors your child is holding on to. One of those is learned helplessness.

FOUR

Learned Helplessness

What Is Learned Helplessness?

Learned helplessness is the habit of children always expecting help because they believe they cannot do a task on their own. Because of this belief, they stop trying. Such behavior results from caregivers helping too much beyond the stage when the children are small and need help with everything.

Most children start rejecting help because of their competence or pride. They like the feeling of mastery. Mastering a difficult task brings a sense of accomplishment, which leads to increasing maturity and independence. However, some children do not break out of their shells and do not insist on doing things themselves. The result is a belief that they are incompetent. Repetition makes this habit an entrenched pattern. But remember—patterns can be changed. Here are some examples and recommendations.

Inability to Complete Homework

Tom has a habit of procrastinating on his homework despite having a set homework schedule. The following is a typical after-school conversation:

You: "Tom, get started on your homework."

Tom: "I don't know how to do it."

Tom stares at his worksheet but does not pick up a pencil.

You: "I'm busy with dinner and can't help you right now. Try to do it yourself."

Tom: "OK."

Tom picks up the pencil and writes his name at the top of the page.

After dinner, you sit down to help Tom with the homework.

You: You sigh. "Let me read the instructions and see what you need to do."

Tom sits silently, waiting for you to dictate the homework. This pattern has been in place for six years.

Recommendation

A behavior chart is best for handling Tom, who waited for you to do the homework. Chapter 21 provides a more detailed explanation of homework wars, as well as additional recommendations.

Example of Wanting Help to Get a Toy

Two-year-old Lee is a late walker. He struggles to stand up and is unsteady on his feet. At this moment, he is sitting on the floor, arms stretched out, fussing. You are busy and cannot pick him up right now.

You: "Just a minute, Lee. I'm busy right now. You have to wait."

Lee: "*Waaaaaaa! Waaaaa!*"

You: "I'm coming! What do you want?"

Lee: Lee points to a toy on the coffee table.

You: "Get the toy yourself. You can do it."

Lee: "*Waaaaa!*"

You know Lee is unsteady on his legs and is afraid of

falling. You get down on all fours and demonstrate crawling to the coffee table.

You: "See? You can crawl and get the toy."

Lee: "*Waaaaaaaaa!*"

The phone rings. It's an important call.

You: "Oh, OK. Here you are."

Recommendation

Let Lee get frustrated and be loud and angry. Anger produces excess energy. Wait and see what he does next. Take your call in a quiet part of the house or yard. When you have more time, see what happens when you avoid helping. Whip your phone out and start filming when he does something to get the toy. Show the video to him and everyone else who might come over—in his presence.

But My Child Is Disabled

The previous example was of a child who has some developmental delays. Lee becomes easily frustrated and cries. You feel bad for him and want to be a kind parent. You want to strike a balance between helping and encouraging independence. Until now, Lee has resisted your attempts to make him less dependent on you. You are now in a repeating pattern.

Like all people, disabled children have personality styles. Some are naturally more independent, and others are just the opposite. Some are passive, some are demanding, some are determined, and others give up easily. As a parent, you want to consider their personality style and encourage as much independence as possible.

Being disabled is tough. When tasks are challenging, we tend to put things off or avoid doing them. In life, disabled children have to work harder than their able peers at everything. For children with disabilities, this means more repetitions to gain a skill, frequent failures and frustrations, and less free time for the caregivers and the child.

The Use of Helplessness to Manipulate Others

Some kids feel incompetent and helpless and decide they don't want to work so hard. They claim incompetence to avoid doing some tasks or to manipulate others to do them. The challenge is getting such children to work harder and experience success so that they can enjoy the feelings of mastery and independence.

The Remedy for Learned Helplessness

Naturally, you do not want your child to feel incompetent, depressed, or anxious. As you set out to work on changing any habits of learned helplessness, keep a watchful eye on your interactions with your child. Attempt to break any interaction patterns that support the learned helplessness attitude. Next, you can find various examples of how to do it.

If your child acts like he is beaten down by life and asks for help with everything, you can compliment him on the smallest ventures and encourage him to do new things by himself. You can use the shaping method, as in the following example.

Example of How to React as Your Child Attempts Independence

Tony has problems with muscle coordination. Usually, he sticks to you like Velcro. At the park, you see him heading up the stairs to the upper level of the playground equipment. He's never shown interest in the stairs before. Your heart is in your throat. You imagine him tumbling down and hitting his head. You want to rush to protect him.

Instead, you find your phone and film him.

You: "I didn't know you can do that!"
Tony stands on the fifth step, unsure of what to do, then sits down. You go to him and show him the video of himself climbing.

22

You: "Look at this video. This is Tony climbing the stairs. We'll have to show the video to Aunt Lilly later. I'll call Grandma to tell her how you climbed the steps all by yourself."
You send the video to Aunt Lilly and Grandma—and the phone rings.

You: "Hello?"
"It's Grandma! She saw the video of you climbing the stairs."
You put the phone near Tony's ear so that he can hear Grandma talk about how he made it to the fifth step.

There are things you can do to increase the self-confidence of children who have developed a habit of helplessness.

Example of Increasing Confidence in a Special Skill Set

You know that Ash, your seven-year-old, is good with computer searches.

You: "Ash, I need your help. Can you show me how to search for a YouTube video on baking chocolate cupcakes?"

Ash: "Chocolate cupcakes? Sure."
He closes the game on his iPad and finds the YouTube video for chocolate cupcakes.

You: "I was watching to see how you searched, but I can't seem to do it on my iPad."
You feign incompetence.

Ash: Ash tries to grab your iPad to search for you.

You: "Show me on your iPad. I want to learn how to do it by myself."
You are using modeling so that he can copy the behavior in the future.

Later, at dinner, you tell the family how Ash helped you

23

find the YouTube video for making chocolate cupcakes. And yes, the chocolate cupcakes were amazing.

Example of a Child Who Doesn't Want to Work So Hard

Ida has developed a pattern of manipulating everyone into "helping," which becomes "doing the work for her."

Ida, Dad, and Mom are in the living room. Dad is catching up on emails, Mom is on her device looking at Instagram postings by friends and family, and Ida is watching TV. Both parents are tired from a hard day at work and helping Ida with her homework.

Ida: "Dad, can you hand me the remote?"
Dad gets up, hands the remote to Ida, and returns to his emails.

Ida: "Thank you. Mom, can you get me a drink?"

Mom: Mom looks up, still under the spell of her sister's vacation photos. "What?"

Ida: "Can you get me a drink? I'm thirsty."

Mom: "OK." She gets up and goes to the refrigerator. "What would you like?"

Ida: "What do we have?"
Mom lists the drinks and brings the one Ida asked for.

This is an example of a repeating pattern in their household. The parents are so busy and tired that they don't notice they are in a pattern. They do all the work, and Ida does nothing.

Recommendation

Call a family meeting. Inform eleven-year-old Ida that she is old enough to do certain things for herself. Give her examples of what you want her to do independently. Make a behavior chart and assign rewards for "Doing things by myself."

Pay attention to what happens when you are with Ida. Old behaviors you want gone will spike before they fade as Ida attempts to return to the old pattern.

A few days after the family discussion, Mom is busy cleaning the kitchen after dinner. Ida is watching TV in the living room.

Ida: "Mom, can you get me a drink?"
Mom: "Get it yourself."
Ida: "But you're already next to the refrigerator!"
Mom: "Remember our discussion? Get it yourself."
Ida: "I'm not thirsty."

Example of a Toddler Who Insists on Being Carried

Ava is an engaging toddler who insists on being carried everywhere despite being able to walk, climb, and run. She is getting bigger and heavier to carry. You and Ava have arrived at the store parking lot. You undo Ava's seat belt and invite her to get out of the car by herself.

You: "Come on, Ava. You're a big girl; you can get out of the car yourself."
Ava: "No."
You: "I know you can get out by yourself. Come on now."
Ava: "Waaaa!"
You: "Oh, OK."
       You get Ava out of the car and stand her on the ground. You offer your hand to Ava.
You: "Here, hold my hand. Let's go to the store."
Ava: Ava refuses your hand and stretches her arms up. "Up!"
You: "My back hurts. Try walking this time."
Ava: "Up!"

You: "Try walking this time."

Ava: "Waaaa! Waaaa! Waaaa!"

You: You sigh. "Oh, OK." You pick Ava up, and she stops crying.

Recommendation

Ava is too young for behavior charts. Instead, you study the pattern of behavior between Ava and yourself and set out to break the habit. It takes time but is worth the trouble and the noise, which will undoubtedly be part of the shift to more independent behavior. Ava has the lungs of an opera singer.

To break the pattern, watch for the tiniest hint of independence, then take videos and share them with your child and others in the family. Everyone in the family can ooh and aah at Ava's independent actions. In this instance, you are using the shaping method.

Each time you arrive home from somewhere, give Ava a chance to get out of the car seat by herself. Whip out your phone, ready to film Ava getting out of her car seat. If she gets out of the car, keep filming as she walks into the house. Show the video to Ava and everyone in the family.

If Ava refuses, get busy taking the groceries out of the car. Clean out the car. Clean out your glove compartment. Ignore Ava until she gets out of her car seat. Only then do you pull out your phone to film. Make sure Ava only gets your attention by doing what you ask.

Now that Ava is good at getting in and out of the car by herself at home, you attempt to take her shopping. Hopefully, Ava has developed a new habit of getting out of the car and walking by your side. If not, you might see a spike in the old behavior of crying and demanding to be picked up. If Ava refuses to get out herself, you pull out your phone and start filming. By now, recording on your phone may have become a trigger for desired behaviors. Say, "I'm waiting." Ava might fall in line, get out of her seat, and walk. If not, stand there and catch up on your messages. Wait for her to get out. Call a friend or a family member and talk to them about what a big girl Ava is. She can now get out of her car seat and out of the car by herself. She can walk to the store and is good about holding your hand. Do not pick her up! You are breaking the pattern.

Learned Helplessness Leads to Dependency

When children grow up believing they are incompetent and need help with each new task, they come across as dependent and helpless. Typically, people are glad to help and guide until they notice that the child expects lots of feedback for every little step. Some people react to incompetence with impatience and complete the task themselves. Others turn away and find someone else to do the task. Such reactions cement the child's belief that they are incompetent, leading to anxiety and depression.

Dependent, helpless children may find a few strong-willed friends who do not mind having a dependent person for a buddy. The forceful friends do not bother to ask their tagalong friends what they want to do. The dependent friend is allowed to participate in their activities, many of which are of no interest to them. Eventually, the dependent kids resent their overbearing friends because they have no power in the relationship. They are not viewed as equals and do not get to choose independently.

You may wonder, *Why don't they speak up and say what they want?* Not speaking up is part of the learned helplessness and dependency package. The dependent children expect everyone to read their minds as their caretakers have done throughout the years. It is up to the caretakers to foster independence.

Until now, we have focused on behavior patterns. It's time to consider how family communication patterns lead to undesirable behaviors.

FIVE

Your Child's Communication Style

Conversations include verbal content, body language, and voice inflection. Body language and voice inflection broadcast our underlying attitudes and emotions about the content. Let's use the words *thank you* as an example:

- Thank you. (Soft voice, eyes lowered, not making eye contact, body at rest)
- *Thank* you! (Lively voice, eye contact, smile)
- Thank *you!* (Body agitated, turning away from you, voice angry, no eye contact). The *thank you* here means the opposite, like "Thanks for nothing."
- *Thank you!* (Big smile, booming voice, eye contact)
- Thank you.(Eye rolling, no smile, sarcastic tone)

Amazingly, these two words can have so many meanings. But that's not all. Some communication styles are interpreted differently in different societies. In the first example, the soft voice and lowered eyes are considered respectful in some Asian cultures. In American culture, no eye contact is considered rude. The second example of lively voice and eye contact is considered appropriate in American culture but may be interpreted as a rude or combative attitude in some Asian cultures.

In this chapter, we focus on American culture. Speaking with the eyes lowered can mean shyness, extreme anxiety, or "I wish you'd go away and leave me alone." The person on the receiving end of this action perceives being shut out. They interpret such behavior to mean you do not want to interact with them. When you walk up to a counter for some service and the person does not look up, you feel like you don't exist.

What does that have to do with your children? Children must learn the nuances of communication. Some are naturally good at it, and some need your help.

Please note that children with autism have a more challenging time with all these concepts because they don't read body language well. If you try to teach them to look at people while they're talking, they have a hard time organizing their thoughts. Many must choose between making eye contact or participating in a conversation; they cannot do both simultaneously.

Body Language

Body language cues such as lowered eyes and turning your back on someone mean, "Go away and leave me alone." Some children use rejecting body language to communicate to others that they do not wish to interact. After a while, the other kids stop trying to be friendly and inclusive. The children who seem to avoid and ignore others are timid and anxious, yet they feel lonely and uncomfortable in social situations. Although such behavior is frequently part of autism spectrum disorder, shyness or lack of eye contact does not mean that your child has autism. They can just be painfully shy.

How to Help Your Child Change His Body Language

You are at the playground and notice your five-year-old, Ken, playing alone, avoiding other children. When another boy approaches him, he turns his back to the child. Sometimes the other child runs off in a different direction; sometimes he pushes Ken or grabs whatever Ken's playing with to get a reaction. Yes, pushing is a type of conversation starter. You decide to talk to Ken about these events at home.

You: "Ken, do you always play by yourself?"

Ken: "Yes."

You: "Even at school? Even when your daddy takes you to the playground?"

Ken: "I play with Daddy."

You: "What about at school? Do you have someone to play with?"

Ken: "No. The other kids are not nice."

You: "All the kids?"

Ken: "I don't know how to play with other kids."

Recommendation

Begin by practicing play and body language with your son.

You: "Let's practice. I'll be Bud."

Ken: "You mean the kid who pushed me on the playground?"

You: "Yes. How did you know his name?"

Ken: "I heard his mom calling, 'Bud, be nice. Don't push!'"
He knew Bud's name, which means that he was aware of the other child. You are happy that he pays attention.

You: "Did you know that when kids feel ignored but don't know how to start a conversation, they might push you or grab your toy?"

Ken: Ken looks surprised. "No, I didn't."

You: "When you talk to me, you look at me and answer my questions. But at the playground, you look down or away from the other kids or turn your back on them."

Ken: "I don't know what to say. I don't know what to do."

You: "Let's start now. I'm Bud. You see me coming in your direction. You turn your body to face me and point your eyes at me."

Ken: "OK."

You: "I have a new bike!"

Ken: Ken looks at you but says nothing.

You: "Why don't you say something like 'Really? Can I see it?' We'll start again. I'm Bud again. I have a new bike!"

Ken: "Really? Can I see it?" (In a flat voice.)

You: "That was very good. Now add some excitement to your voice, like you're excited to see my new bike. Let's do it one more time. I'm Bud again. I have a new bike!"

Ken: "Really! Can I see it?"

You: "Yes! It's over there."

You point and cross the room to the pretend bike. Ken follows you.

Ken: "Cool bike. I wish I had a bike like yours. Can you ride it?"

You: "Yes."

You pretend to ride the bike around the room.

Ken: "Can I try it?"

You: "OK."

Ken: Ken pretends to ride around the room.

You: "You want to climb over there now?"

Ken: "OK."

You: "That's enough practice for today. Tomorrow, we can go to the playground and practice with real kids. Remember, you don't have to be the first to talk. All you do is invite them to talk to you by pointing your eyes at them and turning your body in their direction."

Ken: "Huh?"

You: "Turn your face and belly toward the kid coming to you and look at them. All you have to say is hi. Let them do the talking. You can introduce yourself and ask their name, just like you do with grown-ups."

Tone of Voice and Inflection

Tone of voice and inflection are essential aspects of communication. They telegraph the speaker's emotions and attitude using volume and word emphasis.

- Shy kids worry about angering or offending others. They speak softly, and others may ignore them or push them around.
- Bossy kids speak loudly and demandingly; others may see them as pushy and mean and avoid them.
- Sensitive kids who put on a tough act may speak in a combative manner as if challenging others.

The only time you should worry is when you see a consistent pattern that leads to the inability of your child to make or keep friends or when your child is being bullied or is being the bully.

Other kids react to your child based on their style of communication.

Hitting and Pushing as Conversation Starters

Some kids struggle to start a conversation and find themselves isolated. Sometimes you may see such children hitting or pushing another child as an invitation to play. It certainly gets attention, but not the right kind. But any attention is better than being ignored.

Let's say your child gets pushed or hit out of the blue as a conversation starter. You can teach your child to ask the pusher if he wants to play. You will be amazed by the results.

You can practice at home if your child struggles with conversation starters.

Practice at Home

If you are worried about how your child comes across, you can practice at home. Practice the situations you have observed. This rehearsal helps with future interactions. Practice different tones of voice and inflection with your child. Use action figures or stuffed toys to represent other children, and practice conversations using various tones of voice and inflection.

Example of Conversation Starters

You have observed your Bud (four years old) on the playground. No one seems to want to play with him. They are busy playing with other kids. Bud runs by one of the boys, shoves him, and keeps going. The other boy falls down and then rushes to his mom. You get a look from the mom. Then Bud shoves another boy. The boy gives chase, but Bud is faster. You yell, "Bud, be nice. Don't push!" but then decide to take your son home.

> You: "I was watching you at the playground. You pushed two boys for no reason."
>
> Bud: "They didn't want to play with me."
>
> You: "I did not see you trying to talk to them. You just ran past them and pushed them."
>
> Bud: "I don't know what to say."
>
> You: "OK. Let's practice. Do you know the names of the other boys you pushed?"
>
> Bud: "One of them is Tom."
>
> You: "We can practice inviting kids to play with us."
>
> Bud: "OK."
>
> You: "First, you must know when to start talking to the other kids."
>
> Bud: "I don't know what to say."
>
> You: "Before you say anything, you must be sure they are ready to talk to you. We'll practice with some of your action figures."
>
> To teach attention to body language and knowing what to say, get three stuffed toys, action figures, or dolls. Arrange them so that two are facing each other and the third one is far away.

You: "Let's pretend that these two"—point to the toys facing each other—"are playing. You are standing alone over here. You want to play with them. Walk up to them, then wait until they stop playing and look at you."

Bud: "Huh?"

You: "I'll show you."

Walk the lonely action figure over to the other two. Then move the other two action figures so that they face the lonely figure. "Bud is walking over to where Tom and another kid are playing. Bud has to wait until the other two notice him, stop playing, and point their eyes at him. Now they are ready to listen to Bud. Did you notice how they moved their whole bodies to face the Bud action figure?"

Bud: "Uh-huh."

You: "Now you be Tom and do the talking for him. I will be Bud and talk for you."

Give your son one of the playing figures, and you take the lonely figure.

"I am walking up to Tom and his friend. I want to play with them. I wait till they stop playing and point their eyes at me. Then I ask, 'Can I play with you?'"

Bud: "OK."

You: "Perfect. Let's do it again."

Practice as often as needed for your son to understand the pretend play.

"Was that fun?"

Bud: "Yes."

You: "Let's do it again. This time you'll be Bud, and I'll be Tom."

Practice with the action figures until you are sure Bud understands the concept of waiting to speak until the other figures notice him, stop playing, and turn their bodies toward his action figure. Practice until he remembers to ask, "Can I play with you?" or "What are you playing?" or "Can I join you?"

We have been focusing on external communication styles and patterns, but we all engage in internal dialogue, including kids. The next chapter explains how thoughts can trip up your kids and what you can do to help them.

SIX

Self-Talk Patterns

Thoughts drive our actions, emotions, and beliefs. Therefore, if we can control our thoughts, we can control our behaviors, feelings, and attitudes. Even people who do things on impulse think before they act. The difference is the time lapse between thought and execution. For most of us, our thoughts are censored by the part of the brain that tells us what is appropriate and what is not. Sometimes we call this self-reflective process a conscience.

Repeated internal thought patterns create beliefs about ourselves and the world around us. The eternal optimist reacts positively to any situation. The eternal pessimist responds negatively to the same situation and expects the worst outcome. Our thoughts create our reality. We can convince ourselves that we are terrific, no good, intelligent, dumb, strong, or weak, no matter how others see us. Think of it as internal advertising.

Repetition of ideas, whether internal or in advertising, convinces us that our beliefs are solid. We assume advertising works because companies track whether it increases sales. Commercials appear repeatedly. Repeated messages stick in our heads and become part of our thinking.

What story are you telling yourself? Analyze your thoughts about your self-belief. Notice that you use the same pattern or sequence of thoughts and memories to create the belief. Is this self-belief correct? Probably not, but you feel sure of its accuracy. Sometimes you want to change your perceptions but feel stuck in the self-assessment.

But you're not stuck. You can change your thoughts. They are *your* thoughts. You are in charge! You can change your attitude about yourself, and so can your child.

Negative Self-Talk Can Derail Your Child

You don't have access to your child's innermost thoughts, but you can tell when something is off by their mood or behaviors. Negative self-talk can affect your child in the following ways:

- It increases anxiety states, which manifest as refusals, tantrums, shaking, crying, or shutting down.

- It increases anger, which appears as yelling, throwing objects, hitting, scratching, or biting.

- It increases depression, which appears as withdrawal, crying, food refusal, or self-destructive behaviors.

- It leads to feelings of entitlement and is shown by rude, demanding, and demeaning behaviors.

- It creates the belief that they are terrible at some subject or sport, resulting in comments like "I hate math!" or "I hate baseball." These negative thoughts can lead to reduced effort and avoiding certain problem areas.

How can you, as a parent, help your child change their thinking patterns? The following examples deal with entitled behaviors and the "I hate math!" attitude. Anger, depression, and anxiety are discussed in chapters 29, 30, and 31, respectively.

Example of an Entitled and Superior Child

You love your daughter and are proud of her. She learns easily and is good at sports. However, she tends to put on an air of superiority, and it is affecting her friendships. The following conversation illustrates an attempt to change her habit of superiority:

Meg: "I hate all the kids and teachers at my school. Can I change schools?"

You: "What happened?"

Meg: "Nothing. Don't try to make me think it's my fault."

You: "What happened today that made you want to change schools?"

Meg: "They're all so stupid!"

You: "Uh-huh. I'm listening."

Meg: "Miss Wilkins was doing a math problem on the board, and I told her there was an easier way. She said she wants the class to do it her way. It's so dumb doing all those extra steps for nothing. I told her so."

You: "Uh-huh. What about your friend Lisa?"

Meg: "She's not my friend anymore."

You: "For keeps?"

Meg: "I think so. She's dumb like the others."

You: "How do you know it's for keeps?"

Meg: "She said she doesn't want to sit with me at lunch anymore. She said she was tired of me putting her other friends down and not wanting to sit with them."

You: "Uh-huh."

Meg: "I don't understand why she wants to hang out with them. They're so dumb!"

You: "Are they really dumb, or are you just not interested in what they talk about?"

Meg: "They just talk about their stupid Instagram posts."

You: "Do you think the teachers and kids at a new school would be any better?"

Meg: Meg hesitates. "I don't know."

Recommendation

You tell a story about yourself or a mythical friend. An entitled child can absorb the lesson presented as a story without the need to preach and correct their behavior.

You: "I remember when I was in school. I went through a phase when I thought I was better than the teachers and the kids."

You reframe her self-belief as a passing stage in her life.

Meg: "Really? Did you have to change schools?"

You: "No, I didn't. My mother explained that learning was easier for me than for my friends but that it didn't make me special. It just meant it was easier—that's all. Later, maybe next year, she said, I might come up against a subject that was hard for me and easy for everyone else."

Meg: "Did you think you were better?"

You: "Yes, I did! But I was wrong. I lost my best friend because I was rude to her."

Meg: "What happened then?"

You: "My mother explained that I created a belief in my mind that I was better than others by repeating to myself that I was smarter than the other kids in class. She said I would have more friends when I stopped thinking I was better and realized that everyone is smart in some way and has special gifts."

Meg: "Is what Grandma said true?"

You: "Yes. When I stopped telling myself everyone was dumb, I looked for things they were good at. The three girls I thought were dumb were very good at some things."

Meg: "Like what?"

You: "One was good at playing the piano. The other made beautiful drawings, and another was good at ballet."

Meg: "Like your friend Suzanne?"

You: "Yes. Suzanne and I have been friends since elementary school."

Meg: "She's the girl you used to think was dumb?"

You: "Yes."

Meg: "What did you do? How did you fix things?"

You: "My mother made me apologize to my friend and to the other girls."

Meg: "What did you have to say?"

You: "I had to tell them I was sorry for putting them down."

Meg: "Did it work?"

You: "Not right away. I had to keep trying by complimenting them on things. Their feelings were pretty hurt."

Meg: "What do you mean?"

You: "My mother told me I needed to pay close attention to what they did well. Or if I liked what they were wearing or their hair, to compliment them and say it looked pretty."

Meg: "I don't care about that stuff."

You: "But these girls might. You might also like it someday, even if you don't care about it now. For now, you can look to see if they have special skills you admire and compliment them by saying, 'Wow, I wish I could do that.'"

Example of "I Hate Math!"

In cases like this, you teach the thought-stopping and thought-replacement method. You identify your child's negative thoughts, stop them in their tracks, and replace them with their opposites.

Ann: "I need help with this math homework!"

You: "OK. I'll help you after I finish replying to these emails."

Ann: "*I hate math!*"

You: Typing.

Ann: "I don't even know why we need math!"

You: Typing.

Ann: "I'm so dumb in math."

You: Typing.

Ann: "I wish we had more science classes instead."

You: "OK, I'm done. Let's see what you need to do here. Didn't your teacher explain it?"

Ann: "Yes, but I didn't get it."

You: "Were you paying attention?"

Ann: "I think so."

You help Ann with her math homework. As you explain how to solve the problem, you notice she is not paying attention. You ask her to focus on what you are saying and have her repeat what you said. After some resistance, she can focus and complete her homework.

You: "I want to talk to you about your attitude toward math."

Ann: "I finished my homework. I want to talk to my friends."

You: "It won't take long, but it's important. I figured out why you hate math all of a sudden. You used to enjoy it when you were younger."

Ann: "Yes. I used to be good at math then."

You: "That's it, exactly. But since then, you have convinced yourself that you're no good at math and have stopped trying."

Ann: "Huh?"

You: "When you convince yourself that you're bad at something, you stop listening. It feels like a door slams, and no new information can come in. Then you stop learning. When you stop learning, you get behind."

Ann: "I guess. Can I go now?"

You: "Not yet. Would you like to be good at math again?"

Ann: "Sure. You're not going to send me to some special math class after school, are you? Timmy's parents make him go to tutoring, and he hates it."

You: "No, it's much easier than that."

Ann: "OK. What, then?"

You: "You created a belief that you are bad at math by repeating to yourself that you hate math and don't get it. To undo those beliefs, try this:

- You replace the 'I hate math' thought by telling yourself, 'I love math. I'm good at math.'
- Whenever you think of math, tell yourself, 'I love math. I'm good at math.'
- When you see your math teacher in the hallway, tell yourself, 'I love math. I'm good at math.'
- When you sit down in math class, tell yourself, 'I love math. I'm good at math.'
- When you sit down to do your homework, tell yourself, 'I love math. I'm good at math.'"

Ann: "Will that fix my math problem?"

You: "I think so. You have to clear your mind of the thoughts that you hate math and are bad at math and replace them with the opposite. The change will keep the door in your brain from slamming shut. You will be able to learn again."

Ann: "OK, I'll try it, but why do I need to know all this math?"

You: "Remember how you said you love science and wish you could take more science classes? Well, math is the language of science."

Ann: "Huh?"

You: "When you study science in more detail, you'll discover you need math equations to solve interesting problems and make discoveries and predictions. But for now, you must learn to control your thoughts by insisting you love math."

Ann: "OK, but it sounds kind of crazy."

Storytelling and suggestions help children learn new behaviors and ways of thinking. However, these methods may not work for all children. Some kids insist on being in charge from a very young age and engage in frequent power struggles.

SEVEN

Power Struggles

Power struggles are all about controlling the situation. If you are a forceful parent and want to be in charge, you have experienced many tug-of-wars with your child. A passive parent lets the child have their way to avoid conflict.

Three Styles of Power Struggles

You may recognize the three styles of child behavior in the following examples. Can you identify the passive and sneaky, loud protest, and passive-aggressive styles as the children attempt to gain control of the situation?

Example of Refusal to Use the Toilet

Sometimes power struggles revolve around the use of toilets. Your Sally is a well-behaved girl with an issue concerning using the bathroom, and she hates being reminded. Here is a typical exchange:

You: "Sally, go to the bathroom before we leave for the store."
Sally: "I don't have to go."

Half an hour later, you notice Sally dancing in place at the store.

You: "Do you have to use the restroom?"

Sally: "No."

You: "You look like you have to go. It's half an hour before we get home."

Sally: "I don't have to go!"

At home, Sally hides her soiled underwear.

Recommendation

Sally does not like to be reminded of going to the bathroom, yet she must develop good voiding habits. Realizing that you have a controlling child, you can use modeling to get around the power struggle.

You: "It's almost time to go to the store. I'll use the restroom before we go."

Sally: "I don't have to go."

Sally is trying to get you back into a familiar conversation.

You: "OK."

At the store, you ignore Sally as she dances in place.

You: "I need to use the restroom. It's half an hour before we get back home."

Sally: "I don't have to go."

To break up the old power-struggle habit of bathroom wars, you repeat the modeling behavior so that Sally can develop her own rhythm of going to the bathroom. The old habit of resisting fades away because the idea is no longer your command. Going to the toilet becomes her idea.

Example of Refusal to Pick Up Toys

Jack does not like picking up toys. He is playing in his room, surrounded by all of his toys. The floor looks like a trash dump made up of toys.

You: "Jack, clean up your toys. We have to go to the school to pick up your brother."

Jack: "*Noooooo!*"

You: "I said, pick up these toys now!"

Jack: "Why do I have to?" Crying, whining, winding up for a major showdown.

You: "Because I asked you to."

Jack: Loud tantrum.

Recommendation

Jack's behavior of sitting in the middle of a pile of toys is best handled by behavior charts. Many power struggles occur because someone insists that something needs to be done right now. You want Jack to develop a habit of picking up his toys. Developing the habit is more important than doing so right this minute. Use the behavior chart, discussed in chapter 12, to encourage him to do so and get around the power struggle.

Example of Food Refusal

Food refusal is a common power struggle issue. Here is an example of a typical dinnertime conversation:

You: "Mia, come eat. Dinner is ready."

Mia: "I'm not hungry."

You: "Come. Sit with us anyway. Just remember, there is no dessert if you don't eat dinner."

Mia: "What's for dessert?" Mia sits down.

You: "Chocolate pudding."

Mia: "Are we having broccoli casserole again?"

You: "Yes."

Mia: "You know I don't like broccoli casserole! Can I have a hot dog instead?"

You: "No. I'm not making different meals for each of us."

Dad: "You eat what your mom cooked for us!"

Mia sits sullenly throughout the meal and does not touch her plate.

You: "Everyone else is done. You sit here until you finish everything on your plate."

Mia: "I have to go to the bathroom."

You: "OK, but come right back and finish your dinner."

An hour later, Mia is still in the bathroom.

You: "Mia, get out of the bathroom and finish your dinner."

Mia: "I'm not hungry."

Mia sits at the dinner table until bedtime. She does not eat that night.

Recommendation

Mia picked family dinners as her battleground. Here is another way of handling the same situation.

You: "Mia, come eat. Dinner is ready."

Mia: "I'm not hungry."

You: "Come. Sit with us anyway."

Mia: "What's for dessert?" Mia sits down.

You: "Chocolate pudding."

Mia: "Are we having broccoli casserole again?"

You: "Yes."

Mia: "You know I don't like broccoli casserole! Can I have a hot dog instead?"

You: "No, dear. That reminds me. Guess who I saw today at the store? Vanessa's mom. She said Vanessa misses you and wants to get together. Would you like to get together?" You break the old conversation pattern by deflecting with a distraction by talking about anything except the food on the table. If Mia does not eat her food and everyone is done . . .

You: "Can we share your food?"

You can get around the power struggle by not repeating your part and by changing the subject. Make sure the conversation at the dinner table involves Mia and is about things she enjoys talking about. Mia will try to get you into the familiar pattern for several days but will drop her behavior if you change your approach and do not engage.

What Gives Rise to Power Struggles?

Determined, strong-willed children generally have at least one equally controlling parent or grandparent. Such an attitude is a personality style. The battles for control happen between the strong-willed members of the family.

You think you have a bratty child. Your child believes you are pushy and unreasonable. Your child is not bratty. You are not pushy or unreasonable. You are both controlling.

The good news is that determination will help your child get what they want in life. Their motto is "Never give up." Isn't that your motto? Did it work for you?

Your challenge is to teach them how to use the trait without trampling on others. They have to be taught when to push back on the limits and when to do what they're asked to do. Some family situations result in pitched battles.

Everyday Situations That Illustrate Power Struggles

Here is a list of the most common situations that lead to confrontations. Battles begin in the preverbal stage, when children understand language but cannot speak yet.

- Picky eater: spitting food, refusing food, pointing to other food

- Refusal to carry out a request: crawling away, ignoring caregiver, running off, doing something else, doing the opposite, crying, hitting, scratching, throwing objects, and saying no

- Potty training: refusing to wear a diaper, refusing to sit on the potty, not depositing anything in the potty, soiling the diaper right after the parent put a fresh one on

- Refusing to go to the bathroom when the caregiver suggests going potty

- Nighttime routine: Refusing to go to bed, refusing a bath, refusing to brush teeth, trying to keep you in the room with requests for reading books or back rubs, claiming "I'm thirsty"

- Morning routine: refusing to get dressed, refusing breakfast, refusing to brush teeth and comb hair

- Behavior at the store: loud demands for toys or candy, refusing to get into the shopping cart, refusing to get out of the shopping cart, running off

- Interrupting when parents are talking

- Correcting parents

- Homework wars: refusing to start homework, not allowing homework to be reviewed by the parent, failing to turn homework in, forgetting to write assignments in the planner

- Debating: preteens trying to get a yes by presenting "reasonable" arguments until you get a headache

Strife and Drama

Over the years, I've seen countless families locked in combat. They came to therapy with the idea that one of them was correct and everyone else in the family was wrong. Each expected me to side with them.

Can each of them be right? Yes and no, but who is right is not the point. The issue is past patterns of interaction, which are then repeated time and again to create a familiar conflict. The solution is to change the pattern.

Behavior charts are your most effective tool for overcoming power struggles with your child. You want certain behaviors to become habits. If you list them on a behavior chart, your child does the behaviors to get the rewards, not because you said so. The chart takes you out of the equation and gets around the power struggle.

These approaches work for older kids. What about toddlers?

Nighttime Routine

Bedtime is a frequent battleground, especially if you do not yet have a routine.

Young children thrive on structure. They feel the calmest and are most cooperative when they know what comes next and what comes after. Having a familiar pattern is comforting for them, so create a nighttime routine schedule. Toddlers require one with pictures. If your child resists doing the next thing on the schedule, you can show them the schedule.

Chapter 23 provides an example of how to handle this battle of wills.

Morning Routine

The morning routine is a frequent battlefield for school-age kids. The parents are buzzing around trying to prepare for work and expect the kids to get themselves ready. Some do, but others pick this time to get your attention by stalling, arguing over clothes, watching TV, or fighting with siblings. The result is a loud screaming match every morning—leaving everyone in a bad mood.

Chapter 22 discusses what gives rise to this type of strife and provides recommendations.

Behavior at the Store

Some parents avoid taking their kids shopping because they cause such an uproar. Displays of unruly, loud, and demanding behaviors cause the parents to become stressed, angry, and embarrassed.

Interestingly, children who generally behave well might pick the store as the stage for their horrible-kids act.

Shopping with kids requires a lot of preparation and forethought. Chapter 24 discusses possible reasons for the behaviors and gives tips on changing them.

Homework Wars

Homework wars are brutal. The kids and the parents are worn out from school and work and would love nothing better than to sit and relax. However, homework has to be completed and checked, and dinner has to be cooked. Behavior charts can handle most homework issues.

Homework wars are common and may have other causes besides power struggles. To find out more, please read chapter 21.

Debating, Interrupting, and Correcting

Debating is a form of power struggle disguised as a "logical" discussion. From the kids' perspective, the essential purpose is to distract and confuse you so that they can either get you off their back or get a yes answer.

Debating is a common preteen ploy and is annoying to parents. Your preteen often approaches you with requests when you're dead tired or half-asleep.

Repetitive interruption of conversations is an attention-grabbing device. A child behaving in such a manner can benefit from an intervention with a behavior chart. An in-the-moment intervention can recognize such action as a ploy for attention.

The behavior of correcting parents appears when your child tries to avoid a request with passive avoidance, deflecting, and correcting. Such behavior is best handled with an intervention using a behavior chart. Chapter 25 provides examples and recommendations.

As your child grows older, they develop greater self-awareness. Sometimes you have to help them be more self-aware.

EIGHT

Self-Awareness

Self-awareness ranges from extreme self-awareness to not being aware at all. Kids who are too self-aware become so wrapped up in themselves that they develop social issues because all their focus is turned inward. They feel overwhelmed and unable to focus on others. Psychotherapy can help.

Overly Self-Aware Children

Overly self-aware children observe themselves hypercritically as they interact with others. Such self-monitoring leads to anxiety, which becomes a habit over time. In therapy, children are taught how to remove the anxiety and the hypercritical self-assessment. The next step is teaching them guided imagery to tackle the anxiety about going into social situations. Guided imagery is simply imagining a situation and working on your anxiety to remove the expectation of becoming anxious at a similar event.

Guided imagery is straightforward; you can learn it to help your child with social anxiety.

Example of Guided Imagery to Control Anxiety

Kim refuses to go to her best friend's birthday party because she fears becoming anxious around the other kids.

You:	"You were looking forward to Jane's party."
Kim:	"Yes, I was, but now I feel nervous about it."
You:	"Do you think Jane will be upset about you not coming?"
Kim:	"Probably. She's not good at conversation. I always help her out."
You:	"What do you do when you get nervous at school?"
Kim:	"I do the slow breathing. I start in the car on the way to school."
You:	"I have an idea. You can do the slow breathing now while you imagine going to the party. Keep breathing slowly while you imagine getting into the car. Imagine breathing slowly in the car until you are no longer anxious. Then imagine yourself walking into Jane's house while doing the slow breathing. Keep breathing slowly as you imagine yourself giving her the present."
Kim:	Kim's breathing speeds up.
You:	"Check your breathing and slow it down."
Kim:	"OK."
You:	"What are you imagining now?"
Kim:	"I'm going into her house."
You:	"Whenever you feel nervous, check your breathing and slow it down. Go back to the part where you didn't feel nervous. Even if you go back to the car in our driveway."
	Sit silently and wait for Kim to finish the exercise in her imagination. Whenever her breathing gets faster, stop her and ask where she is in the process. Remind her to slow her breathing down.
Kim:	Big, slow sigh. "I think I can do it now."

You: "Great. Let's do this exercise over again. Just remember to breathe slowly all the time. You'll do great."

Kim: "OK."

Chapter 17 describes how to teach your child slow and even breathing, which is an excellent tool for reducing anxiety and anger.

Lack of Self-Awareness in Children

Lack of self-awareness can create many social problems for children. If it is severe, your child will be shunned by peers and considered a problem by adults. Here is an example of what you can do to help your child develop self-awareness.

Jim has trouble making friends. He walks up to the kids and starts talking about something unrelated to what they are discussing. The kids look at him and then turn away and shut him out. No one wants to play with him. The rejection has been going on for months. Now Jim walks around with a mad look on his face. You have been teaching him to pay attention to the conversation and to listen without blurting. The two of you have also been working on turn-taking.

Jim looks angry and feels angry because he expects rejection. When his teacher asks him why he's angry, he says he's not. You decide to have a discussion with Jim to help him become aware of his feelings and let go of his anger.

You: "Jim, your teacher told me you walk around angry all day."

Jim: "No, I don't!"

You: "You're making a mad face right now."

Jim: "No, I'm not."

You: "Let's go to the mirror. What do you see? A happy face?"

Jim: "No."

You: "A sad face?"

Jim: "No."

You: "How do you feel inside right now?"

Jim: "I'm mad 'cause you're making me do this stupid stuff."

You: "So your mad face matches how you feel inside?"

Jim: "Yes."

You: "Is this how you feel at school?"

Jim: "Yes."

You: "What is going on at school that makes you angry?"

Jim: "I'm trying to talk to the other kids. I plan to do what you taught me, but they turn their backs on me when they see me and walk away."

You: "I'm so sorry. It must hurt your feelings a lot. You've been working so hard to be a good friend, but now you don't have a chance to practice. Maybe they don't realize you're different now, or your mad face makes them walk away. I can email your teacher to ask if she has any ideas."

Jim: "I don't think it'll help. She doesn't like me either."

You: "I didn't get any complaints from the teacher. Are you staying in your seat and doing your work without disturbing the other students?"

Jim: "Yes."

You: "I'll discuss all that with your teacher. Right now, we need to get rid of the angry feelings and the mad face. Do you remember how we use slow breathing to do this?"

Jim: "Yes. But why do I have to get rid of the anger?"

You: "Does anger feel good inside?"

Jim: "No."

You: "Do you like being around me or Dad when we get angry?"

Jim: "No."

You: "What do you do when you see us angry?"

Jim: "Go to my room."

You: "That's right; you don't want to be around us. Do you see why the other kids might not want to be around you when you're angry?"

Jim: "I guess."

You: "Let's do the slow breathing now to get rid of those bad feelings. Remember to let go of some angry feelings every time you breathe out."

Recommendation

In this example, you acknowledged your child's hurt and anger. You explained how his emotions affect others and how they react to him. Now you want to teach your child to let go of old hurts and anger so that he can move forward. Holding grudges and holding on to anger do not feel good inside and damage relationships.

Chapter 17 has a more thorough description of the breathing process explained here.

PART 2

Parental Interventions

NINE

How to Mold New Behaviors

Part 2 of this book is devoted to interventions you can use as a parent to encourage new behaviors and extinguish undesirable ones. You may be more familiar with some techniques than others. I expect you will implement the ones that suit your personality style. Perhaps you had been using one of them, but it stopped working—or it never worked. This could be because it didn't suit your child's personality style. You may want to experiment with something else.

Common Ways to Teach New Behaviors

Modeling means demonstrating the behavior and asking your child to copy you. In truth, everything you do from morning to night is considered modeling because children naturally copy their parents.

Shaping refers to encouraging new or complex behaviors you are attempting to teach. Instead of expecting your child to copy entire sequences of behavior, you reward any effort in the direction of such action. As a parent, you can use the shaping method with small children. Coaches use shaping in sports. You can find examples of shaping in chapter 3.

Reinforcing desired behaviors refers to using rewards to encourage certain behaviors. The rewards can be a smile, an encouraging comment, or an elaborate reward system such as a behavior chart. Chapters 11 and 12 provide more details.

Your Reaction to Behaviors Matters a Lot

Your reaction to behaviors matters, whether you are attempting to teach a new behavior or replace an old habit.

In chapter 10, I classify parent reactions as positive, negative, and inconsistent. Positive reactions work best for creating new behavior patterns because they are essentially positive attention, which your child craves.

If you are inconsistent with your reactions to your child's behavior, you are practicing intermittent reinforcement. Your child will be confused about what you want and how to get your attention, resulting in the persistence of the behaviors you don't like.

Consistency is the key.

We'll start with the basis of all new behaviors—getting your child's attention.

Doing What You Ask the First Time You Ask

Focus on the behavior you want to instill in your child as a starting point—for example, doing what you ask the first time you ask.

For best results, start with preferred activities when you begin the training. Preferred activities include eating, going to the park, or watching TV with you. Nonpreferred activities include brushing teeth, doing homework, picking up toys, and bedtime.

Getting your child's attention before you attempt to teach a behavior is very important.

Example of a Request to Stop Playing

Make sure your child is in the same room and is making eye contact with you.

You: "Joey."
Joey: Joey averts his eyes and ignores you.
You: You move closer to Joey and repeat, "Joey."

If the child is hyperactive, is autistic, or has slow processing, you might have to call his name and wait thirty seconds for your request to sink in.

If the child still avoids looking at you and keeps doing what he's been doing, take his face in your hands and repeat his name.

You: "Joey."
Joey: Joey looks up.
You: You smile. "Are you hungry? Dinner is ready."
Joey: "Yes."
You: "Come and eat."

For the learning to stick, you have to repeat the sequence many times to the point of overlearning.

Example of an Issue with Transitions

Some children have problems with transitions (moving from one activity to another) and kick up a fuss even if you offer to transition to a preferred activity.

Stay with your child. Just stand there. See what your child is doing. Do not leave the room. If the child continues playing, then hold out your hand.

You: "It's time to go eat."

I use the phrase "It's time to [go, eat, get up, sit down]" because the expression works so well with hyperactive kids and those on the autism spectrum.

If Joey goes back to building a tower, for example, you can do the following:

You: "Joey."

Joey: Joey looks up.

You: Your hand is still outstretched. "This is a beautiful tower. It's time to eat now. We're having your favorite food, pizza. When you finish eating, you can come back and work on your tower."

I recommend repeating this sequence with several preferred activities before you expand your practice to nonpreferred activities, such as brushing teeth or doing homework.

You want the phrase "It's time to" to trigger your child to stop, listen to you, and do what you ask when you ask. A trigger can be a phrase or a school bell—something familiar that triggers a behavior transition.

Perhaps you've heard the saying that consistency is the key to getting better cooperation from your child. I said it myself earlier in this chapter. You don't have to smile every time your child washes their hands after a meal until they grow up and leave home, but it does mean that you pay attention to whether they are washing their hands after a meal. Eventually, washing hands becomes a habit after many repetitions of this nonpreferred activity.

Example of Transitioning to a Nonpreferred Activity

You: "Joey, it's time to pick up the toys."

Joey: "*Nooo!*"

You: "I know you want to keep playing, but it's time to pick up the toys."

Joey: Joey does not look at you. "I want to play."

You: "Joey."

Joey: Joey looks up.

You: "It's time to pick up the toys. Tomorrow you can play again."

If your child ignores you, pick him up or walk him away from the toy he was playing with and take him over to another toy that needs to be put away.

You: "It's time to pick up the toys. I can help you."

If Joey does not reach for a toy, stand behind him and take his wrists in your hands. Guide his hands to grip the toy, then walk Joey and the toy to the toy box or the shelf while holding on to his hands with yours.

You: "Good work, Joey! It's time to put the next toy away."

If Joey does not reach for another toy, guide him by the wrists again, as just explained. Once Joey picks up toys and puts them away on his own, you can switch to taking turns.

You: "Good work, Joey! We can take turns. Now it's my turn. Which toy do you want me to put away?" You are giving Joey some control over the situation. "Now it's your turn, Joey. Which toy will you put away?"

If Joey pitches the toy into the corner of the room in a fit of anger, you can say:

You: "That's not where the toy box is. Let's get the toy and gently put it in the toy box." Then walk him over to the toy he just threw.

If you lose patience with the process, you will lose the training message. Joey will learn he can outwait and outwit you if you pick up most of the toys.

Brace yourself for the training process and leave enough time for the most resistant child. Don't delay this important training until your child is a teenager and towers over you. You want them to listen to you and do what you ask when they're still smaller than you.

We turn to consequences when modeling, shaping, and rewards aren't working.

TEN

Punishment and Consequence Styles

Your Reactions to Behaviors Matter

This chapter is about behaviors your child has already learned. You want to encourage some behaviors and get rid of others. Young children depend on you for attention and getting things they want, such as food and toys. They repeat annoying behaviors, such as whining or getting loud and demanding, only because the actions worked before when you gave in to their demands to stop the noise.

Experience has shown that positive reinforcement (rewards) works better than negative reinforcement (consequences) to increase desired behaviors. Focusing on the positive makes behavior charts the ideal tool for increasing the occurrence of behaviors you want to see more of. Behavior charts are discussed in chapter 12. First, we need to understand what forces keep undesirable behaviors resistant to correction efforts.

Parent reactions are the key!

Table 1 lists common parental reactions to their children's behaviors.

Intermittent reinforcement (inconsistent reactions) leads to the tightest bond with the behavior. Inconsistent responses to your child's behavior will keep the unwanted behaviors going forever.

Take gambling as an example. You keep doing the same behavior, and sometimes you get rewarded with a win, but most of the time, you don't. Another example of intermittent reinforcement (consequences) is video games. Sometimes you get rewarded with a win and sometimes not. There is always more to win and a different way to win.

You display intermittent reinforcement if you are inconsistent in your reactions to your child's behavior. The child is unsure if you want to see more of those behaviors. They assume the behavior is OK if you're in a good mood but not if you're cranky.

How Have You Been Dealing with Unwanted Behaviors?

Children know their parents and know how far they can push. Here are three examples of parent reactions to problem behaviors:

1. The parent ignores the behavior because they are busy.

2. The parent finds themselves explaining the reasoning behind their request repeatedly but without any change in their child's behavior.

3. The parent repeats the request several times without results. The parent loses patience and yells. The child acts when the parent's voice gets to the decibel level where the child knows that bad things will happen to them.

If these descriptions sound familiar, it's because you're not alone. Parents who work from home frequently encounter the first issue. Remember, kids are all about attention. If you're busy and can't interrupt your train of thought, they try positive behaviors first, and if that doesn't work, they'll engage in behaviors they know get your attention.

Table 1. Parental Reactions

Parent Reaction	Type of Reaction
Positive reinforcement	Smile, praise, clapping, or rewards
Negative reinforcement	Frown, *the look*, sharp tone, rejecting, ignoring, yelling, time-out, spanking, taking things away, shaming, comparing to siblings
Intermittent reinforcement	Rewarding the desired behavior sometimes and ignoring it other times; punishing unwanted behavior one time but letting it slide the next

Parents who explain, as in the second issue, create a pattern of giving their undivided attention to their child by explaining. The child then tries to keep the explanations going simply because they were successful in their quest for attention. The two of you then develop a pattern over time.

The third issue is the most common. Your child ignoring your request is most likely due to a pattern you've developed over time. In rare cases, the child has a hearing problem, or language processing impairment. Hyperactive kids have attention problems. However, because you expect them not to hear, they learn to pretend they don't hear to get out of fulfilling requests. The fake inattention becomes a game or a power struggle.

Consequences and Punishment

Each parent has their go-to corrective behavior. Table 2 describes common parental reactions and lists the reasons why I recommend or do not recommend such interventions.

The next chapter deals with the most effective ways to correct behaviors.

Table 2. Typical Parental Reactions to Misbehaviors

Parent Reaction	Description	Recommend?
The look	Frowning, *the look*, or saying the child's name in a sharp tone all convey a "Stop what you're doing right now" message.	Yes
Rejecting actions	Rejection can be verbal or nonverbal, including rolling your eyes and turning your back on the child or saying, "You can't come to the baseball game because you hit your brother."	No
Ignoring	You ignore the behavior and the child.	No
Yelling	Yelling gets some of your frustrations out and might frighten the child, but it is not helpful in changing the behavior. Losing your temper makes you look like you're out of control and therefore not to be taken seriously. Because children copy the behaviors of their parents, you end up with a child who yells.	No
Time-out	Time-outs are a cooling-off period for the child to calm down when they get worked up or angry.	Yes
Spanking	Spanking, not beating, might work when the child is small. One "pop" with your hand on their bottom might hit their reset button, but there are more effective ways to change behavior, so I am not recommending hitting. Older kids just get mad and become silently rebellious. Hitting takes the focus away from what you are trying to correct.	No
Taking things away	Taking prized possessions or privileges away is effective if done with forethought and consistency.	Yes
Shaming	Shaming creates other issues and is not effective in changing behavior, so I definitely do not recommend put-down comments. For those who are not sure what shaming is, here are some examples: "How can you be so stupid?" or "What's wrong with you? I just showed you how to do it!" This response vents your frustrations, but that's all.	No
Comparing	Comparing comments—such as "Why can't you be like your brother?" or "Why can't you be like Johnny?"—make the child feel unloved and the brother or sister triumphant. There will be no behavior change.	No

ELEVEN

How to Effectively Correct Behaviors

These are my recommendations and examples of the methods I consider most effective.

Frowning, *the Look*, or Saying the Child's Name in a Sharp Tone

Many parents talk to their children in a calm and even tone. Such a manner of speaking fails to convey to the child when you're serious or just chatting.

Spoken communication consists of the content of what you say, your body language, and your tone of voice. What you say is less significant than how you say it and what you do with your facial expression, body, and voice inflection.

When correcting your child, change your body language, tone of voice, and facial expressions so that they know you mean business. I recommend practicing looking angry and sounding stern before you get mad. It's best to practice in front of the mirror to see the difference.

Training yourself to change your tone saves you time and trouble. Here is an example of one such practice.

Practicing a Stern Facial Expression and Manner of Speaking

Find a mirror and watch yourself say, "Jake. Please stop" in your usual manner. Then knit your brows or raise an eyebrow and say, "Jake. Stop." Next, try using a stern voice and an angry facial expression, saying, "Jake! Stop." Can you tell the difference? I recommend practicing several times, using various phrases until you're good at it. Use the new tone when you want your child to stop what they're doing.

Notice how your child reacts to the new you.

Two-year-old kids love to test limits. It usually looks funny and adorable, but you want to train them to stop in their tracks when you say no sternly. They do not know enough about the world and can easily wander into the street, get run over, stick their fingers in the shredder, and so on.

Time-Out

Time-outs are popular because they stop the pattern of what is going on and help everyone calm down.

For little ones, pick a spot for their time-out. You can call the time-out location the quiet spot. It can be a chair, rug, or stair close to where you are. You don't want separation anxiety to kick in by putting them in their room. Have your little ones clasp their hands together. Grab a kitchen timer, or use the timer on your phone.

You: "It's time to calm down. Sit down in your quiet spot, put your hands together like this, be quiet, and keep your body calm until the timer rings."

Demonstrate putting your hands together as if in prayer, then moving your fingers between each other into a clasped-hands position.

Both the timer and the clasped hands are important. The timer lets you and the child know when the time is up. The timer becomes the reinforcer, the reward, to let your child know they succeeded in staying calm for that amount of time.

Clasped hands are super essential for hyperactive kids with difficulty sitting still. The hands become an anchor for them to stay in one place. Once the hands are apart, they wander. Soon you have an extended arm, and the rest of the body follows.

Set the time-out minutes by age. The easiest rule of thumb is one minute for each year of life. For example, set the timer for three minutes for your three-year-old and ten minutes for your ten-year-old.

When your child gets older, you can move time-outs to their room. If they are into power struggles with you, they might pop out of their room to ask, "Is it time yet?" Tell them you are restarting the timer, and they are not to come out until you come for them. If you have been conscientious about sticking to the timer, and they know you're not just getting rid of them, the behavior will stop.

The Benefits of Time-Outs

Ideally, you want your child to behave without any punishment. Time-outs are good training for children to help create a new internal habit of calming down. When they feel worked up about something, they need to separate themselves from the situation and take the time to calm down and sort things out.

When I worked with kids and parents, I spent much time explaining what time-outs are for. Instead of talking about punishment, I explained that a time-out is a time to calm down. I told the children that grown-ups take time-outs without being told. Then I said, "You know, you don't have to wait to get in trouble to take a time-out. You can tell your mom or dad, 'I need a time-out.' Then go take a time-out until you calm down."

Use this statement as a teaching moment to help your child moderate their emotions.

Please don't use time-outs to give yourself a break from the kids. Sometimes when parents have had it with persistent misbehavior, they send the kids to their room without a specified time to come out and then leave them there for a long time. I understand your frustration, but sending them to their room for a long time will not improve their behavior. Instead, such treatment makes them feel ignored and rejected. You aim to avoid rejecting them and give them the attention they crave instead.

Behavior charts work wonders if set up and applied correctly. They are a form of parental reaction involving a reward system for several behaviors simultaneously.

TWELVE

Behavior Charts

Why Behavior Charts?

Did I hear you groan? You tried behavior charts and then gave up on them. Why does everyone keep talking about behavior charts?

Because they work—if done correctly.

A busy home is filled with confusion. Many parents work from home and try to manage work and childcare themselves. The TV is on, computers are open, phones are ringing, the children and pets are clamoring for attention, and the parents are worn out and tired. All are overstimulated and overwhelmed. As parents try to manage their kids' behaviors in a calm manner, the children may have a hard time knowing when the parents mean business.

Behavior charts bring order to the home. Before you present your kids with a behavior chart, discuss the desired behaviors with them so that they know what is expected of them.

For best results, limit yourself to five behaviors you want to see more of.

Setting up behavior charts helps parents decide what behaviors to focus on right now. The children find the charts an excellent way to know what their parents are noticing and what to do to get rewards. Most kids like to earn rewards instead of doing a behavior just because you said to. The charts work wonders in circumventing power struggles.

Behavior charts are also a great way to instill new behavior habits in your kids. You keep the behavior chart going until your child is successful 100 percent of the time. The long duration gives the new behavior time to become second nature.

What Behaviors Are Listed on Behavior Charts?

Through the years, I've worked with many parents on behavior charts. The main mistake most make is to put the behaviors they want stopped on the chart. Please avoid focusing on behaviors you want to disappear. Aren't those the behaviors your child was doing to get your attention in the first place? Yes, yelling is a way of getting attention. You do not want to see those behaviors, so do not put them on the chart. Instead of *yelling*, you write *quiet voice*.

I recommend you tell your child what you want to see more of, then pay attention when they engage in those behaviors. Putting the desired behaviors on the chart and giving positive points for them is a much more powerful way of effecting behavior change. Giving points or minutes becomes the reward.

Confused? Read on. Lots of examples follow. I provide lists of desired behaviors, how to assign the points or stars, and examples of how a behavior chart looks. I've included a list of desired behaviors for older kids, and there are examples of picture equivalents for the younger ones who cannot read.

The Most Common Behaviors Listed on Behavior Charts

- *Do what I ask the first time I ask:* This item is essential because it prevents arguments. Being able to do this behavior requires that your child pay attention to you, stop what they are doing, and do what you ask. (They will earn forty points for doing so without reminders, twenty points for one reminder, and zero points for more than one reminder.)

- *Brush teeth, get dressed, and comb hair before breakfast:* Parents complain that their young ones play or sit in a stupor in the morning instead of getting dressed. (They will earn twenty points for doing the behaviors without reminders, ten points for one reminder, and zero points for having to be reminded more than once.)

- *Calm voice, calm body:* Some children have meltdowns and screaming fits that can bring the roof down. They throw tantrums with minimal provocation, such as when you say no to something they ask for. They've learned that if they pitch a major fit, you will let them have what they want just to shut them up. Give points for staying calm all day. (They will earn twenty points for doing so without reminders, ten points for one reminder, and zero points for more than one reminder.)

- *Avoid correcting/arguing:* Some kids like to correct their parents and become argumentative instead of doing what is asked of them. Instead of taking points away for arguing, give points if they avoid correcting and arguing. (They will earn twenty points for doing so without reminders, ten points for having to be reminded one time, and zero points for having to be reminded more than once.)

- *Put toys/phone/tablet away:* Give points and praise to your child for picking toys up and putting them away. (They will earn ten points for doing so without reminders, five points for having to be reminded once, and zero points for having to be reminded more than once.)

- *Share toys:* Instead of punishing them for grabbing toys for themselves, give them points for sharing. (They will earn ten points for doing so without reminders, five points for having to be reminded once, and zero points for having to be reminded more than once.)

- *Play nicely:* Give points to your child for getting along and avoiding fights and arguments with siblings and friends. (They will earn twenty points for doing so without reminders, ten points for having to be reminded once, and zero points for having to be reminded more than once.)

- *Remember to write down homework assignments:* Some children forget "accidentally, on purpose" to write down their homework assignments. Give them points for remembering to do so. (They can earn twenty points for writing down their homework assignments. No reminders for this item.)

- *Finish homework before play:* Some children use homework to get your attention. To foster independence, you can use the behavior chart to give them positive attention for completing their homework independently. (They will earn ten points for doing so without reminders, five points for having to be reminded one time, and zero points for having to be reminded more than once.)

- *Turn in your homework to the teacher:* Some parents battle with their kids over homework every night and confirm the homework was done, only to find out that their kids did not turn it in. If your child is playing that game, don't worry about the reason. Include the desired behavior as previously stated. If all homework is done electronically, they must show you it's been submitted. Give points for handing the work in. (They can earn twenty points for handing homework to the teacher or submitting it electronically before class. There are no partial points for this item.)

- *Calm yourself down and take time to cool off:* Some children get angry quickly and need to learn self-soothing and self-calming techniques. Most kids are familiar with the concept of time-out. Teach your kids to take their own time-outs to calm down instead of waiting until they blow up and get a time-out from you. Explain that they can give themselves time-outs before they get into trouble. That's what grown-ups do. (They will earn twenty points for doing so without reminders, ten points for having to be reminded one time, and zero points for having to be reminded more than once.)

Setting Up a Behavior Chart

You can use my charts as examples. I recommend using Excel because you can copy, modify, reuse, and reprint them. Table 3 shows how you can list the desired behaviors on the left side and include the total points in a box at the end. Put the days of the week on the top. Make sure that your chart has gridlines before you print it out. Once the behavior chart is printed, you can enter the points earned each day with a pen or pencil. You can print the same chart for the following week. Please retain and compare the charts from week to week so that your children can see their progress.

Each night, spend time with your children to record their scores. Make sure you calculate the total at the end of the week. The points can be exchanged for small toys or money. Older kids can trade the points for minutes of game time or on other electronic devices. You know what motivates your kids the most. Make each point equal a penny or a minute of game time. The penny/minute system is easy to calculate. Little ones who do not know how to add enjoy stars instead of points, as in table 5. You can draw the stars or use stickers.

Please note that I assigned more points for some behaviors in the following examples. I based my points on the effort required to accomplish those behaviors. The definition of *effort* depends on your child. Some kids hang on to behaviors because they suit their personality style. Others may struggle to do the listed behaviors. If you sense any blockage or resistance, give more points for that behavior.

The behavior charts with written behaviors are for readers. You can draw or paste pictures to represent the desired behaviors of little ones. For example, you can put a picture of a stop sign for the behavior "Stop, look, and listen." Brushing teeth and getting dressed can be represented by a picture of a toothbrush and a shirt. A calm body and voice can be represented by a finger across the lips for *shush*. Sharing toys can be represented by a picture of one child offering a toy to another. Putting toys away can be substituted by a toy box, as shown in table 5. If you cannot think of an image to represent a particular behavior, keep the behavior off the chart until you find a way. Children who use stars on their charts can earn a maximum of three stars. Everything needs to be simplified.

Tables 3, 4, and 5 are examples of behavior charts to give you an idea of how yours might look once constructed.

Examples of Weekly Behavior Charts

Table 3 is an example of a weekly behavior chart and the points earned for each behavior. Your behavior chart should have a maximum of five behaviors, as in tables 4 and 5. You want to pick the most important behaviors to change. When your child masters those, you can create a new behavior chart with other behaviors they struggle with. Table 3 has many items to help illustrate what words you can use to convey desired behaviors.

Rewards

Some kids are motivated by money, some by special outings, some by toys, and others by electronic devices. The points and stars can be converted to the rewards your child will work the hardest for. For example, your preteen may want game time during the week. This can be earned by converting the points to minutes. Your youngest one may want to get an action figure or a doll. In this case, they get one if they earn a certain number of stars.

Updating Behavior Charts

When your child consistently accomplishes the listed behaviors, you may want them to acquire some other new habits. Make a new behavior chart to specify those additional behaviors.

Table 3. Examples of Desired Behaviors, Possible Points, and Points Earned

Behavior	Possible Points per Day	Mon	Tue	Wed	Thurs	Fri	Sat	Sun	Weekly Total
Do what I ask the first time	40	0	0	0	20	20	20	40	
Stop, look, and listen	40	0	0	20	20	0	20	0	
Brush teeth, dress, and comb hair	20	0	10	10	0	10	0	10	
Calm body, calm voice	20	10	0	20	0	10	20	20	
Take time to cool off	20	0	20	10	10	0	20	20	
Avoid arguing	20	0	0	0	0	0	10	10	
Share toys	10	5	10	0	0	5	5	0	
Put toys away	10	5	5	5	10	10	10	5	
Play nice	20	0	10	0	10	20	20	10	
Assignment written down	10	10	0	10	0	0	0	0	
Homework completed	10	10	0	10	5	0	0	0	
Homework handed in	10	0	10	0	10	10	0	0	
Total		40	65	85	85	85	125	105	590

Siblings

Because behavior charts carry rewards, siblings can feel left out. Even if your other kids are perfect angels, consider finding some behaviors they can improve and make behavior charts for them. You'll be amazed by the results.

If your children tend to argue and fight, and you want this to stop, put it on their behavior charts. At the end of the week, give them big bonus points for a perfect, strife-free week. On the chart, you can list this as "Getting along all week." They will be motivated to work together to get the bonus.

Chore Lists

Some parents put chores on the behavior chart. Please avoid doing so. You can make separate chore charts. After a few weeks of behavior charts, your kids will develop new habits. You can retire the behavior charts until another set of problems arises. Chore lists have a different purpose and last much longer.

Why Behavior Charts Fail

A behavior chart can fail even if you create it using my recommendations. The most common reason for failure is inconsistency in completing it each night. Children crave your approval and attention. If you don't take the time to sit down with them to discuss their behavior and assign the points for that day, they assume you don't care that much.

Constructing behavior charts and reviewing the behavior and points each night is a time-consuming process. As you're grumbling, please remember the time savings and the peaceful household you can gain if you stick with the behavior charts. It's worth it.

Table 4. Example of a Chart with Five Behaviors

Behavior	Possible Points per Day	Mon	Tue	Wed	Thurs	Fri	Sat	Sun	Weekly Total
Do what I ask the first time	40								
Avoid correcting/ arguing	20								
Assignment written down	10								
Homework completed	10								
Homework handed in	10								
Total									

Table 5. Example of a Picture Behavior Chart

★ ★ ★	Mon	Tue	Wed	Thu	Fri	Sat	Sun

Undermining the Parents

Some parents and caretakers get into power struggles with each other, leading to a contest about who is the better parent. One of the parents or grandparents wants to show that they can get the child to comply by bribing him.

Please explain to everyone who cares for your child that the point of the behavior chart is to develop good behavior habits so that these actions become second nature. Please avoid getting into a contest about who is the better parent. Your child is in training to be a pleasant, cooperative, self-directed, and self-sufficient adult.

Behavior charts are great, but there are other ways of managing behaviors.

THIRTEEN

Use of Storytelling to Manage Behaviors and Fears

Storytelling works well with bossy kids who hate being told what to do. The stories can be about other children, princes and princesses, or animals struggling with similar crises, behaviors, emotions, or self-control issues. Every story contains a main character who reacts like your child to a life event. The main character tries to solve their problem. After false starts, they find the right solution. Of course, the perfect solution in the story is what you want your child to do.

Example of Regressing to Babyish Behaviors

Your son, who has been potty trained for two years, started to wet the bed after the birth of his sister. You want him to return to waking up with a dry bed. Here is a story that fits this example of regression caused by jealousy.

> Prince Tony lived in a big castle with his mommy, the queen, and his daddy, the king. They had several servants, and Prince Tony had many toys. He was the only prince in the kingdom,

and everyone paid attention to him. One day, the queen told him he would soon have a little brother or sister. Prince Tony was happy that he would have someone to play with.

The day arrived when Princess Ann came to live with them. Everyone in the kingdom came to bring the princess presents. People who saw the princess said she was beautiful.

No one paid attention to Prince Tony anymore. The king, queen, and servants were busy with the princess and the visitors who came to see her. Prince Tony felt very sad. Finally, he was allowed to see her. She was tiny, bald, ugly, and noisy. She cried a lot and was loud. Prince Tony felt cheated. "I can't play with her! She's too small! She can't even walk!"

The king said, "She'll get bigger, and before you know it, she'll be able to play with you."

Prince Tony went back to his room. Now he was sad and mad. The princess was just a baby, and no one had time for him. He wished he were small again. Prince Tony thought, *Maybe people only like babies and not big kids. Maybe they'll like me again if I start acting like the princess.*

So Prince Tony started crying a lot for no reason, like the princess. He began to wet the bed, like the princess. But that did not work. He got attention, but it was different from the attention the princess got. The king and queen acted disappointed and mad. The servants gave him angry looks.

As Prince Tony started getting desperate, the king came to his playroom one day. The king sat Prince Tony on his knee, just like he used to do before the princess came to live with them. The king looked worried. "Is there something wrong, my little prince? You have changed since Princess Ann came to live with us."

Prince Tony told the king, "I thought I was getting a prince or princess I could play with now. Since Princess Ann came, no one has paid attention to me; no one has brought me presents, and everyone told me to be a big boy. I feel lonely, sad, and angry."

The king said, "When you were born, the same thing happened. The whole kingdom celebrated, and you got lots of presents. You don't remember all the attention because you were so small. I understand why you feel ignored and unloved, and I'm sorry. I will talk to the queen. We will spend more time with you. But you still have to wait for your sister to get bigger so that you can play with her."

The solution embedded in the story is for the boy to tell his parents what he is feeling. What is he sad or mad about?

Example of First-Day-of-School Anxiety

Your little girl can't wait to go to kindergarten. She's been excited about school all summer and wanted to shop for a lunch box and school supplies like the big kids.

Two days before the start of school, she said she didn't feel well and didn't think she'd be able to go to school. You assume she's worried about something and ask what is bothering her. She denies being worried. You decide to tell her a story.

Cindy was so excited about going to school with the big kids. But she became worried when it was almost time to start the school year. Cindy worried she wouldn't know what to do in school. She wouldn't know where to go. The school is big. She might get lost. She wouldn't know what to do in class. Cindy likes to be good at everything, but how can you be good at something you don't know? Cindy was so worried about all these things that she felt sick. She hoped Mommy would keep her home.

Mommy took Cindy's temperature and told her she didn't have a fever. Mommy said, "You look worried." Cindy kept saying she felt sick inside.

That night, Cindy couldn't fall asleep because she was worried about school. Finally, an idea popped into her head. *I* can ask Veronica questions about school. She's going into first grade and was in kindergarten last year!

The next day, Cindy asked her mommy to invite Veronica over. When Veronica came, Cindy asked, "What happened on the first day of kindergarten?"

Veronica said, "I don't remember much except that I was nervous because I didn't know what would happen or what I was supposed to do."

Cindy asked, "Did you get lost?"

Veronica replied, "No. Mommy helped me find where I was supposed to go."

Cindy asked, "Is kindergarten hard? How do you know what to do?"

Veronica said, "The teacher is nice and kind. She tells you where to sit and what to do. That's all I remember."

Cindy asked, "What if you have to go to the bathroom?"

Veronica explained, "You raise your hand like this, wait for the teacher to call your name, and then say you need to use the restroom. You can ask Miss Smith down the street if you have more questions. She's a kindergarten teacher."

Mommy came in and offered them a snack. Cindy told her mommy about Miss Smith and asked if she could talk to her. Mommy said, "Sure. I'll talk to her first and ask if it's OK."

After lunch, Mommy took Cindy to visit Miss Smith. Cindy asked what happened on the first day of school in kindergarten.

Miss Smith said, "The teacher stays with you the whole time and explains everything. Your mommy can help you find the classroom. The teacher tells you where to put your lunch box and coat. Then the teacher tells you where to sit. You have lots of time to look around the classroom at all the pictures and the supplies. We spend time getting to know one another. You might see some kids you know from your neighborhood. You learn your teacher's name, and the teacher has to learn the students' names. If the teacher asks you to draw, she explains where to get the paper and the crayons. Then the teacher goes around the classroom to make sure all the children understand what to do. When she finds a confused student, she explains what to do until the student understands. The teacher also explains what you will be learning all year. Don't worry if you don't understand. She repeats everything. Please remember that all the students are new to the school. No one knows what to do."

Cindy had a big smile on her face. All her worries went away. She said, "Thank you, Miss Smith," and went home with her mommy. She couldn't wait to start school.

The solution embedded in the story is to ask questions if you're worried about something. If you don't get the answer from one person, find someone else to ask.

Storytelling works well with younger kids. You can use this technique with your older children if you are a natural storyteller. If stories are not your forte, you can use conversations. You can find many examples of conversations throughout the book.

Conversations and storytelling are also helpful in teaching children about feelings and how to express them.

FOURTEEN

Feelings and Emotions

Feelings and *emotions* are words used to describe the same thing. We read other people's emotions through their facial expressions, body language, what they say, and their tone of voice. Identifying and naming what you feel inside is essential to self-awareness. Recognition of feelings and self-awareness are the building blocks of emotional regulation.

1. You must be able to recognize and name what is going on inside you.
2. You attempt to control your reactions to what you are feeling.
3. You become aware of what you feel and how you come across.
4. Once you form self-awareness, you can begin to learn emotional regulation.

Some children develop emotional recognition and self-awareness intuitively by watching the adults around them. Others must be taught how to recognize and name feelings in order to become self-aware.

Parents Are in Charge of Teaching About Feelings

I'm sure you have been teaching about feelings as you speak to your child.

- You explain how their actions or what they say makes you feel.

- When they say something unkind to another child, you explain that what they said hurt the other kid's feelings.

- When you see your child being emotional, you name the feelings.

- You teach feeling words by guessing at your child's emotions.

- Their facial expressions, their body language, the words they use, and the volume of their voice help you guess.

- If the face of your autistic child does not reveal the turmoil inside, you may learn other signs, such as a tense body, an increase in self-calming behaviors (stimming), a flushed face, or restlessness.

- The situation that caused the emotions helps you guess what they're experiencing.

You do not have to teach what *happy* or *embarrassed* means. Instead, include the feeling words in the conversation as you speak about everyday things. If your child asks what the word means, then you try to explain by using a situation familiar to your child.

Example of How to Explain a Feeling Word to Your Child

You: "Were you *embarrassed* when I talked about your drawing with your teacher?"

Sam: "Huh?"

You: "*Embarrassed* is a feeling word. You feel uncomfortable and hot inside. You wish I had not said anything about it because you were not proud of your drawing. You can feel your cheeks getting hot. You wanted to hide somewhere."

Notice I did not use the word *ashamed*, just in case Sam does not know the word.

Example of How to Insert Feeling Words into a Conversation

Sam is delighted because there is a lot of snow on the ground. He is ready to rush out in his pajamas.

You: "Sam, I know you are *excited* about the snow, but wait to get dressed and put on your jacket and boots. It is very cold outside."

Sam: Sam is getting dressed in the warm house. "I'm hot."

You: "It will be cold outside."

Sam: After playing in the snow, Sam takes his mittens off to throw snowballs. "My hands are cold."

You: "Yes, the snow is cold. Almost as cold as ice. Let me know when you're ready to come inside."
The sun comes out at lunchtime, and the snow melts. Sam looks out the window at the disappearing snow. He looks sad.

Sam: "The snow is going away. Will it snow again tonight?"

You: "I'm not sure."
The phone rings. It's Grandma.

You: "Hello, Grandma. Yes, Sam was so *excited* when he saw the snow this morning that he was ready to rush out in his pajamas. Now he is *disappointed* the snow is melting. He looks so *sad.*" Long pause. "Yes, we stayed out there a long time. He finally came inside when his hands got cold. It was too long for me. I'm *exhausted.* I hope he doesn't catch a cold . . . Oh, that is so thoughtful of you." You turn to Sam. "Sam, Grandma is coming over with some hot chicken soup. She's *afraid* we'll get sick from staying out so long, and she says a blizzard is coming."

Sam: Sam smiles. "Now I'm *happy* again. Do you think we'll have enough snow to make a snowman?"

You: "If the blizzard comes, I'm *confident* there will be enough snow."

Sam: "Huh?"

You: "*Confident* means 'sure.' I'm *sure* there will be enough snow."

Grandma pulls into the driveway to deliver her chicken soup.

Sam: "I don't *like* chicken soup."

You: "*Shh.* You'll *hurt* Grandma's feelings."

Gma: "How is my favorite grandson today?"

Sam: "What is that smell?"

Gma: "I know you don't like chicken soup, so I brought a surprise. If you eat the chicken soup, you get to eat the surprise. Why are you giving me a *suspicious* look? Don't you *trust* me?"

Sam: "Huh?"

Gma: "You're looking at me like you think I'm trying to trick you. You don't believe I'll give you the treat."

Sam: Sam sniffs the air. "What's in the box?"

Gma: "Are you *curious* to see what's in the box? I'll show you."

Sam: Sam looks inside the box. It's the biggest cookie he's ever seen. "Wow! That whole cookie is for me?"

You: "Now wait a minute. That's too much for one dessert."

Gma: "Are you *surprised*, Sam?"

Sam: "Yes. Let's eat! I'm *hungry*!"

You: "Grandma, you are so *exasperating*. That's too much sugar for him."

Gma: "I have to go now. I'm *worried* about getting home before the storm hits."

After the meal, Sam watches the weather report.

Sam: "I can't wait for tomorrow. I'm so . . ." Sam yawns.

You: "Are you *bored*?"

Sam: "No. I'm *tired*."

The story shows how you can insert comments about emotions into daily conversations. You can incorporate the following steps into exchanges with your child:

1. Encourage your child to become aware of how he feels and name the emotion.
2. Next, he can talk about the intensity of the feeling. How strong is the feeling inside?
3. Is the emotion too strong and overwhelming?
4. How can he make the feeling less intense?

If you have not mentioned feelings in your conversations before, you can start now. Your goal is to teach emotional regulation. Chapter 8 ("Self-Awareness"), chapter 15 ("Emotional Regulation"), chapter 17 ("Relaxation Technique"), chapter 29 ("Anger"), and chapter 31 ("Generalized Anxiety") provide additional information.

Emotions That Typically Require Emotional Regulation Assistance

Aggression, anger, anxiety, arrogance, depression, desperation, distress, dread, fright, grief, hate, feeling overwhelmed, paranoia, rage, resentment, terror, and withdrawal are all included in this category. You can find tips on how to teach emotional regulation in the next chapter.

FIFTEEN

Emotional Regulation

Emotional regulation refers to the ability to moderate and control one's emotions. No one is born with this skill.

We have to learn how to do the following:

- Stop being overwhelmed by emotions.
- Manage our feelings.
- Express what we feel.
- Keep from overreacting to situations.
- Let go of hurts and disappointments.
- Look at situations from a different perspective.

As parents and caretakers, we are prone to focusing on the excessive display of negative emotions. However, negative emotions that are bottled up and never expressed are just as harmful because they destroy people from the inside.

Parent-child interactions are essential to the development of emotional regulation. If a child is with a caretaker all day, their interactions with that caretaker are also crucial. Because children learn by observing and copying, they also copy the adults' emotional reactions. Table 6 describes three basic parental emotional styles.

Parents Can Teach Emotional Control

Most of the time, kids copy their parents, and things are fine. They develop an emotional range and can identify emotions.

But what if they don't?

Then you teach them.

Children have to learn to identify what they feel before they can control their feelings. Self-awareness and naming feelings must be taught. You can find more information on feelings and emotions in chapter 14. Do the teaching when your child is somewhat calm. No learning can take place when a child is overwhelmed by emotions. The following techniques show how you can help your child during emotional turmoil.

Slow the Breathing Rate

Excessive anger, anxiety, agitation, and impatience all lead to a heightened state of internal excitation. The state of excitation spills over into behaviors. The most common sign of overexcited children is their breathing rate. The breathing rate speeds up, and the breathing becomes shallow. Angry children breathe as if they just ran three miles when, in reality, they've been in the same room with you all the time. Anxious children look as if they're about to start hyperventilating.

Breathing and emotions are intertwined and inseparable. Strong emotions affect your breathing, but the opposite is also true. You can calm your emotional state by controlling your breathing. Slow breathing is your first line of defense. But what if your child is in the middle of a major tantrum and not listening to any directions?

What to Do if Your Child Is Already in the Middle of a Tantrum

- You can start talking to him about slowing his breathing so that he can calm down.

Table 6. Emotional Parent Reactions

Type of Emotional Parent	Parent Behaviors	Not 100% of the Time
Very emotional parents	Yell, hit, throw things, impatient, easily agitated, quick to cry, quick to get anxious.	Initial and immediate reaction. These parents are also able to talk to their kids and explain emotions.
Parents with good emotional regulation	Use words to express emotions. "When you do that, it makes me angry." Or, "When you do that, it makes me sad."	These parents blow up sometimes and yell and get anxious, but overreactions are not the norm.
Parents who do not show emotion	Do not show emotional reactions to events and expect the kids to suppress their emotions.	These parents show emotion some of the time but suppress it quickly or deny their feelings.
Parents under the influence of alcohol or drugs	Behavior ranges from overreacting with emotions to sitting there loaded and ignoring the kids no matter what is going on.	These parents' reactions are directed by what they ingest. They either overreact or act like the kids don't exist.

- Sit down, put him on your lap with his back facing your tummy, cross your arms in front of him, intertwine your fingers with his, and rock slowly back and forth. You start rocking in time to his breathing. Rock forward for each breath out and back for the breath in. After ten times, begin rocking slower. His breathing slows down in rhythm to your rocking. Keep the process going for a long time.

- Keep your voice low. Teach by example. If you want him to lower his volume, demonstrate a lower voice volume. He will follow you. It might take some time.

- You are teaching him how to calm down and teaching yourself how to stay calm at the same time.

Example of a Toddler in Distress

Lee worked himself up to a tantrum while you were on a work call and couldn't stop to help him calm down.

Lee: Lee is kicking his legs and screaming. "*Waaaa! Waaaaa!*"
You: "OK, Lee, I'm here. First, let's calm down."
       You are giving him attention.
Lee: "*Waaaa!*"
You: "It'll be OK. We'll calm down together."
       You pick Lee up. Sit down with him. Put him in your lap with his back to you. He's still kicking and flailing. You intertwine your fingers with his opposite hands so that your arms are crossed in front of him, like in the previous picture. If your hands are big, you can cup your hands over his.
Lee: "*Waaaa!*" Lee is still kicking.
You: "Now we start the slow breathing."
       Slow breathing is also for you because you want to stay calm. At the start, you begin the slow breathing without him following you. When Lee feels you are relaxing, he will relax as well.

Lee: "*Waaaa!*" Lee is squirming.

You: "Very good, Lee. We can slow down together. We put our hands up like this for breathing in and put them down for breathing out."

When you breathe in, raise Lee's hands to his chest; bring them down to his lap when you breathe out.

Lee: "*Waaa!*" Lee is still squirming and kicking sometimes.

You: "Very good, Lee. We are calming down together."

Continue the slower breathing as you move his hands up and down in rhythm.

Lee: "*Waa!*"

You can feel some of the tension leaving Lee's body.

You: "Just like that. Now it's time to take bigger breaths."

You start taking slower, deeper breaths.

Lee: Lee has stopped yelling and squirming. His breathing has slowed down, and his body is relaxed.

You: "We did it. We got calm together. Do you feel better?"

Lee: Lee nods.

You: Take him off your lap so that you are facing him. "You were really upset. Were you angry?"

Lee: Lee nods.

You: "Were you scared?"

Lee: Lee nods. He is small enough to suffer from separation anxiety when he cannot see or hear you.

You: "I'm sorry you felt scared and angry."

In this example, you calmed Lee down and then helped him name his feelings. You were guessing because he is too small to identify his emotions. You guessed the feelings he might have felt based on the circumstances of the situation.

Chapter 29 provides an example of how to calm a child who is yelling and hitting in a fit of anger. Next is another method to try.

A Cold Shower to Combat Emotional Turmoil

You have an early-morning meeting. Typically, you try not to schedule early meetings because your preteen, Kim, is prone to panic attacks. You got up early so as not to rush. Kim got up in a state of agitation. You try not to hurry her, but you are the one taking her to school. Kim begins to feel super anxious.

You: "Kim, I can tell you're getting anxious. Let's stop what we're doing and do slow breathing."

Kim: "OK, but I don't think it will work."
Kim's breathing is short and shallow.

You: You sit across from Kim. "Let's sit on the couch and start." You and Kim do the slow breathing together, but you can tell she's struggling to calm down. You're going to be late for a critical meeting. There is no such thing as "hurry up and relax." You think of something else.

You: "Remember what the doctor told you about shocking your body to reset your emotions?"

Kim: "You mean the cold shower?"

You: "Yes. He said to start with a warm shower and then shut off the hot water to make it cold. It resets your body by shocking it."

Kim: "OK, I'll try anything."
Kim goes into the shower. She comes out shivering.

You: "How do you feel?"

Kim: "Cold. The anxiety is better, but now I'm cold."

You: "I'll get you something hot to drink. Hot chocolate?"

Kim: "Yes."

You and Kim are on the way to school. She'll be late, and you are late, but she feels better. You feel good because you know that she has one more tool to combat her panic attacks.

Transfer of Emotions

Sometimes one emotion appears briefly only to be transformed into another. I've noticed such swaps in people who have been trained to suppress anger. For example, your child feels betrayed by a friend. There is a flash of anger, but then the anger disappears and is replaced by anxiety.

Please reconsider if you have been teaching your child to stuff angry feelings. Instead, help your child give a name to the sensation of anger, sympathize with what caused the feeling, and teach them how to let go of the anger. If the anger is not recognized and dealt with, it will accumulate and destroy your child on the inside.

Ignoring Feelings

Ignoring your child's feelings does not make the emotions go away. Ignoring or minimizing their emotions makes them feel like they're all alone with their accumulated negative feelings. All the feelings they've stuffed over the years might come out at once when they are teens or young adults. Your child might turn to drugs and alcohol to help them make the negative emotions go away. The worst-case scenario can be a suicide or homicide.

I recommend you acknowledge your child's feelings and help them deal with unpleasant or overwhelming emotions.

Teach your child to self-regulate by using relaxation, as described in chapter 17. Relaxation and mindfulness are the most effective techniques you can teach them. When I speak of slow and even breathing, I do not mean "take ten deep breaths." True relaxation involves learning to focus on your body and relax at will. Mindfulness involves paying attention to what is going on inside of you. Teaching slow and even breathing makes you aware of how it works and feels. Do the slow breathing with your child.

Sometimes emotions are tied to impulsivity and flare up before the child can suppress them.

SIXTEEN

Impulsivity

Impulsivity interferes with self-awareness and self-regulation. All children start out impulsive but learn to curb their impetuousness through observation and explanations by parents, teachers, and peers. For example:

- You have to wait your turn.
- Mommy is talking now.
- Use your indoor voice.
- Stay on task.
- Stay in your seat until the bell rings.
- When the teacher is talking, the class has to be quiet.
- Stop, look, and listen before crossing the street.
- I'm not done explaining. Wait until I finish.
- Raise your hand and wait for the teacher to call on you before you speak.
- Read all the instructions before you start to answer the questions.
- No. You have enough toys. We are not shopping for toys.

Most children can learn to curb impulsivity through social learning. Hyperactive children are easily distracted and ignore social cues.

They are impulsive in their thoughts and actions. They can still learn to be less impulsive, but the teaching is repetitive and laborious.

Impulsivity exists even in the absence of hyperactivity. Preteens are in a hurry to grow up, go places, and acquire stuff. You get bombarded with requests all the time. Talk with your child about impulsivity, the importance of curbing their actions, and what they say. Self-control is an essential part of becoming an adult. Here is a way to teach your preteen to be less impulsive:

1. Your child thinks they want to buy something or do something.
2. Teach them to create a wish list first.
3. Teach them to wait two weeks from when they wrote the item down.
4. Most things on the list will be forgotten during the two weeks.
5. If they are remembered, evaluate: Can we afford it? Is this a good thing to do?

You may think these suggestions are simplistic, but they are practical and easy to apply. The list must include the date of the request and the request itself. Post the list in a prominent spot. When you get a new request for something, direct your child to put it on the list.

Your Mia wants new makeup she's seen on social media. Tell her, "Put it on your wish list and wait two weeks. If you still want the makeup, we'll talk about it." By the afternoon, Mia has forgotten all about the makeup and is asking for a new bathing suit.

Mia may skip putting some of the requests on her wish list. Keep your own list of all the requests and when they came in. At the end of the week, show the list to Mia and explain that she came to you sixteen times with new requests. Show her the dates and times. Ask her if she remembers any of them. Chances are, she'll say no.

Explain to her, "Part of growing up is telling yourself to hold off for two weeks when you think you really want to buy something or do something. If it's really important, write it down on your wish list. You will probably forget all about it when it's not in front of you." Ask Mia to use the two-week waiting period before she comes to you with a request.

Most likely, she'll forget and come with new requests. You can redirect her by asking if she put those requests on her wish list and waited two weeks before coming to you.

Working on impulsivity is a long process. Mia's memory is not great. Making the lesson a new internal habit requires a lot of repetition, but this training is essential for her life as an adult.

As with requests for things, some children are subject to sudden, overwhelming, and changeable emotions. This makes their day-to-day life difficult and creates problems within the home and with friends. It makes parenting challenging. Your go-to method is to teach them self-calming techniques so that they can self-soothe when emotions overtake them.

SEVENTEEN

Relaxation Technique

Relaxation techniques, such as slow and even breathing, are perfect for teaching self-regulation and for preventing emotions from overtaking your child.

Follow the description in the next section to learn how to teach the relaxation technique to your child. But before you attempt to teach it, please practice on yourself to become aware of your own reactions. Having the experience will make you a better teacher.

Slow Breathing

To teach slow breathing, pick a time when your child is relaxed. Introduce the idea of learning to relax to get rid of bad feelings. Explain to your child that slow and even breathing can help them when they're feeling mad or nervous. Modeling is most effective, so please do the slow breathing with your child.

Time your child's breathing rate. Anxious or angry people take five seconds or less to breathe in and out one time. Their breathing is short and shallow because the lungs won't expand. I recommend slow and even breathing because when people are overwhelmed with emotion, the muscles around the rib cage tense up. Telling a person to do deep breathing feels like an impossible request. Once they relax, their lungs will expand naturally.

Before you start the breathing exercise, select comfortable seating for each of you. Introduce the process.

You: "We are going to practice slow and even breathing. I'm going to show you my slow breathing first. You try to copy me."

You demonstrate slow breathing (see table 7).

Jim: Jim tries to copy your breathing. You notice Jim holding his breath after he gulps a breath in two seconds. He is holding his breath for two seconds instead of one.

You: "I will match my breathing to yours so that you can follow me more easily."

Match Jim's speed by imitating his breathing rate. Move your hands up from your lap to shoulder height for breathing in, then back to your lap for breathing out. The timing isn't as important as the feeling of increasing relaxation.

Jim: Jim tries to copy your hand movements.

You: "You don't have to do the hands. I was showing you when to start and stop on the breathing in and breathing out."

Jim: "You told me to copy you."

You: "Yes. I did. I will stop doing the hands when we are both breathing together."

Follow Jim's breathing for a few minutes, then slow your breathing a bit. See if Jim can follow comfortably. If not, speed up a bit. You want him to unwind, but relaxation cannot be forced. There's no such thing as "hurry up and relax."

You: "That's good, just like that."

Jim: "How long do we have to do this?"

You: "Until we get good at it and can slow our breathing without holding our breath too long." You stop the hand motions when you see Jim matching your breathing pattern. Keep slowing your breathing down. You want to

Table 7. Approximate Times for Slow-Breathing Demonstration

You can start with: 3 seconds in 1-second break 3 seconds out 1-second break	Do not use a stopwatch. Just guess. Focus on how you feel inside when you are doing the slow breathing.

be slow but still comfortable. You want Jim to be able to match your breathing. "You're doing well. Just like that."

Jim: Jim yawns.

You: "That's good. You're doing really well. Now close your eyes and pay attention to your shoulders. Your shoulders drop a bit each time you breathe in or each time you breathe out. Take your time to discover when your shoulders drop. Keep breathing slowly. Pay attention to your shoulders as you breathe. Can you tell when your shoulders drop little by little?"

Keep doing it until you and your child feel relaxed and can answer the shoulder question.

Jim: "When I'm breathing out."

You: "Me too. How do you feel?"

Jim: Jim yawns. "Fine." Jim looks relaxed, and his breathing has slowed down.

You: "That's enough for today. We'll practice every day to get really good at relaxing."

Jim: "OK."

Do the slow-breathing exercises almost every evening until you see Jim doing them on his own without being prompted by you. When you see him get worked up about something and notice him shift to slow breathing without reminders, you can be sure that Jim has developed a new habit of self-regulation.

How to Apply Slow and Even Breathing

If your child struggles with emotional control, you can do additional practice when they are in a state of excitation. Such practice creates another habit of slowing down and breathing slowly whenever they feel overwhelmed.

The breathing exercises benefit your child by making them feel as if they have control over their anger or anxiety. Now they have a tool.

If your child struggles with anxiety, you can tell them, "Check your breathing when you feel nervous, and slow it down. You can slow your breathing anywhere: at home, in class, or on the playground. No one will know what you're doing. The breathing is your very own secret."

If your child struggles with anger, you can tell them, "Check your breathing when you feel angry, and slow it down. You can slow your breathing at home, in class, or on the playground. No one will know what you're doing. The breathing is your very own secret."

Once you teach your child the exercises for slow and even breathing, please practice them yourself to reduce your stress level.

PART 3

Frequent Situations Encountered by Parents

EIGHTEEN

I Just Told You Not to Do That!

You just told your son, "Don't throw the rock!" A moment later, he throws the rock.

Why do they do something you just told them not to do? Your child is not a brat, and you're not a bad parent. So why doesn't he listen? Parents came to my psychology practice with their disobedient and willful children. Indeed, there are such children. But yours may not be one of them.

The reason can be a simple communication slip. If so, the fix is easy. The *no* and *don't* get ignored in our thoughts and communications.

The brain reacts as if it didn't hear the no or the don't and just heard a command to do it.

This slipping interferes with the message on the communication level. It happens with adult-to-adult communications and adult-to-kid conversations.

I picked kid examples because we're always telling them what not to do.

- You say: "Johnny, don't touch the stove!" Johnny touches the stove.
- You say: "Johnny, don't jump into the pool!" Johnny jumps into the pool.

- You say: "Susan, no cookies before lunch." Susan gets stuck on cookies before lunch.
- You say: "Johnny, don't pull Susan's hair." Johnny pulls Susan's hair.
- You say: "Don't get out of your seat." The child jumps, falls, or slides out.
- You say: "Don't interrupt while I'm talking." You are interrupted twice.

In these examples, it seems that the kids misbehave intentionally, which can infuriate you. Sometimes they do, but most of the time, the phrasing of the request is to blame.

Something goes wrong with the processing of the *no* and the *don't*.

A fascinating brain quirk is the failure to process negative commands in sentences such as *no* and *don't*. Research on the subject is scarce. However, one study shows that hearing or thinking negative words in a sentence causes the brain to work extra hard, compelling it to interpret the words and then stop the action.

Possibly, the communication is misinterpreted, or the action is initiated before the *don't* is processed. I haven't found the answer, but there is a simple fix.

You may have experienced the solution yourself. Telling others what *to do* can lead to better outcomes.

Don't Tell Them What Not to Do—Tell Them What to Do

You might start by listing all the negative commands you issue to your child during the day on a piece of paper. Then think of alternative ways of phrasing them.

At first, making the change seems unnatural, but you'll soon get the hang of it. You'll be glad you put in the effort when you see the results. Table 8 shows some examples.

Table 8. Turning Negative Statements into Positive Statements

Negative Statement	Positive Statement
Don't touch the stove!	Please stay away from the stove. It's hot!
Don't jump into the pool!	Jake, please use the steps to get into the pool.
No cookies before lunch.	Let's leave the cookies for after lunch.
Don't pull Susan's hair!	Johnny, come here, please. I want to show you something.
Don't interrupt while I'm talking!	Please wait to speak until I'm finished. I will call on you when it's your turn.

You may have noticed in these examples that the action words in the positive statement column differ from those in the negative. *Touch* becomes *stay away, jump* becomes *use the steps*, and so on.

Now replace the negative statements on the list you created with positive ones. In the future, when you want your child to avoid doing something, remember to tell them what you want them to do instead. Beware of the word *don't*.

These examples work at home and at school. However, there are times when children's behavior varies depending on the setting.

NINETEEN

My Child Misbehaves at Home but Is a Perfect Angel at School

If this chapter's title resonates with you, you are not alone. Many other parents share your experience. Perhaps your child feels you don't appreciate good behavior. Maybe you punished them for something they didn't do or broke a promise of a reward. Try talking to your child about the cause of their actions. You might get an answer.

If you get a response that does not make sense or if you get an "I don't know," implement the strategies outlined in chapter 1. Try them for two weeks so that your child can get used to the new you.

Catch Them Being Good

Children crave attention. They try to get your attention by being good, but if that doesn't work, they try other behaviors that get them noticed. Kids will keep trying until you do notice them!

"Catch them being good" is a saying I borrowed from teachers. For example, suppose your child makes one misstep but also shows positive behaviors. You ignore the misstep and compliment them on behaviors you like to see. Examples of such actions are taking a dinner plate back to the sink, putting a cup on the counter instead of throwing it, picking up a toy, or using kind words.

Alternatively, if your child picks up a toy to throw it, you can interrupt the motion by grabbing their hand and saying, "Great picking up!" This confuses them and might prevent an angry outburst.

You can use your phone to take videos of your child doing amazing things, such as picking up their toys, sharing, or playing peacefully. Send the videos to family members whom they love. Prompt the relatives to praise the video. Remember to gossip to Grandma or a friend on the phone about how your young one is acting older every day and how proud you are of them.

Bad Behavior at the Dinner Table

When young children are surrounded by adult conversation, they get bored and feel left out. First, they try to be cute. If that does not get attention, they spill things, eat like a dog, refuse to eat, make themselves bleed, hit a sibling, and so forth. Kids are all about attention.

The remedy for attention-seeking behaviors is remembering to include your child in the conversation by telling the other adults about their accomplishments and new skills. If your child likes to talk, ask them questions about their favorite topics. When the adults speak, maintain occasional eye contact with your child and smile at them when they are well behaved.

If all these strategies fail...

Find Out What Methods of Behavior Control the Teacher Uses

If your child behaves better at school, try to determine why.

- Does the teacher keep a schedule?
- Is every expectation explained clearly?
- Does the teacher have a token or point reward system?

- Does the teacher walk up to the children and guide their hands if they do not respond?
- Try to understand what the teacher does so that you can employ their methods at home.
- Ask the teacher what works for your youngster at school.

Take notes.

Do not give in to pride or shame. You want results, and a meeting with the teacher will be worthwhile. Clearly, your child can behave well; they just choose not to do so at home.

Try the Teacher's System at Home

Try the new system for at least two weeks. Your child will respond because it is familiar. Try it even if it seems like a lot of work. If your child responds positively, the effort is worth every minute of your time.

If you are still experiencing problems, try following the advice in chapter 2 ("Patterns and Habits"), chapter 9 ("How to Mold New Behaviors"), chapter 10 ("Punishment and Consequence Styles"), chapter 11 ("How to Effectively Correct Behaviors"), and chapter 12 ("Behavior Charts").

Some parents experience the opposite problem—children who are perfect angels at home but who misbehave at school.

TWENTY

My Child Misbehaves at School

The last chapter dealt with misbehavior at home but not at school. Now it's time to tackle the opposite problem—the child who is disobedient at school but cooperative at home.

Refusal to cooperate with the teacher can be due to the following factors:

- Boredom
- Power struggle
- Dislike of the teacher
- Attempt to impress peers
- Inability to perform what the teacher requests

A heavy-handed approach does not work here. You must be diplomatic with your child and with the teacher. Your child is struggling with something, and you need to help them navigate a difficult situation.

Here are examples of triggers for such conduct, followed by tips to resolve the problem.

An Attempt to Impress Peers

You open an email from Jim's teacher. As you read the message, your eyes widen, and your heart races.

Dear Ms. X,

At the start of the year, Jim was the perfect student and friend to his classmates. Then something changed. He has become rude, disruptive, and verbally abusive to the other kids. I spoke to him about his behavior and told him it must stop. He doesn't seem remorseful and claims nothing is wrong. The behavior continues.

Has anything changed in his life to account for the transformation in conduct?

Respectfully,
RJM
Sixth-grade language arts teacher

You take deep breaths to calm yourself to avoid overreacting. You are a single mom, but Jim is the same Jim he was during the summer and last year. He likes to spend more time alone than he used to, but he's getting older, so you think keeping to himself is natural. Jim's dad has a new family, but Jim enjoys his visits with his father.

Before speaking with Jim, you call a friend whose kids are older. Your friend shares that her son, Connor, went through a similar stage. Eventually, she found out he had a crush on a girl in the class and was trying to impress her by being a tough guy. The girl was not impressed and began ignoring Connor.

Recommendation

Armed with your friend's experience, you call Jim in for a heart-to-heart.

You: "Jim, I received an email from your language arts teacher describing you as 'rude, disruptive, and verbally abusive toward other students.' Do you behave like this in other classes?"

Jim: "No."

You: "Do you dislike Ms. RJM? You never complained about her."

Jim: "No. She's a good teacher."

You: "Can you explain the behavior, then?"

Jim: "No," says Jim, but he looks embarrassed.

You: "Are you trying to impress someone?"

Jim: Jim looks down and fidgets but says nothing.

You: "I spoke to Connor's mom. She said he went through a similar stage, and it turned out he was trying to impress a girl. It didn't work, and the girl ignored him."

Jim: A blush spreads to Jim's neck, but he says nothing.

You: "You know how I feel about school and about being kind and respectful. Perhaps you can speak with a therapist if you can't tell me what's wrong."

Jim: "No. It's OK. I can stop."

You: "Are you sure you don't need to talk to someone?"

Jim: "I'm sure."

You write an apologetic email to the teacher, mentioning that you spoke to Jim, who assured you he will revert to being respectful and kind.

Your educated guess about the reason for Jim's behavior was correct. A week later, the teacher emails you that whatever magic you used has worked, and Jim is his old self again.

Inability to Perform What the Teacher Requests

Your third grader, Ann, used to be a cooperative student who struggled with reading. Her third-grade teacher believes in helping children overcome their fear of reading aloud by having them do so frequently.

Between Ann's anxiety and reading problems, she complained bitterly about this teacher from the start of the school year.

Today, you receive an email from the teacher.

Dear Ms. A,

Ann has been asking to use the restroom multiple times a day and refusing to read aloud. I've tried talking to her, but she says she can't read aloud.

Can you please speak with her?

Respectfully,

FLN

Third-grade teacher

Recommendation

You know Ann struggles to read aloud or silently. She becomes anxious whenever she feels overwhelmed or faces a situation she cannot escape. At such times, she excuses herself and goes to the bathroom.

Ann had been in therapy for anxiety, and the therapist told you frequent urination can be a sign of anxiety. Ann is not anxious at home and does not use the bathroom excessively. What approach do you use in this situation?

One suggestion is that instead of getting Ann to comply with the teacher's request, you use the teacher's email as an opportunity to ask for a school evaluation of Ann's reading problems.

Write a response to the teacher explaining Ann's struggles with reading and anxiety and request a recommendation for a school evaluation of her reading problems. Also ask for a face-to-face meeting with the teacher to discuss Ann's issues. Before you send the email, copy the school's principal and vice principal.

During the teacher meeting, try to persuade the teacher to stop forcing Ann to read aloud because it makes her so nervous that she cannot focus all day. If the teacher is unmoved by your plea, recap your meeting in an email to the teacher with a copy to the principal and vice principal.

Request a meeting with the principal. Repeat the issues and the request for evaluation. Such evaluations contain test results as well as recommendations. Generally, the psychologist doing the testing sends a form for you to complete. The form requests background information and descriptions of Ann's behavior at home.

When completed, the psychoeducational evaluation will most likely recommend special accommodation and remedial reading support for Ann. Once the accommodation plan is in place, the teacher is mandated to follow it. Ann will be set up for success instead of anxiety.

How Acting Out Is Expressed in Older Kids

Older kids are more likely to act out because of a dislike of the teacher, power struggles, or boredom.

Kids who are well behaved everywhere else respond to a heart-to-heart conversation like this: "You can't expect to like or respect everyone, but you must let them do their job and not interrupt. When you interrupt a teacher, the other students in the class cannot learn, so you're hurting everyone. It's bad manners to show your contempt or dislike of a person. If you're bored, find something to do. Draw or doodle."

If the teacher is bossy, and your child who engages in power struggles develops issues with this teacher, you can remind your child he is bossy himself by saying, "Now you know how it feels when someone behaves as you do. You're not in charge. The teacher is. Stop interrupting and correcting. Let the teacher teach."

Explanations do not cure the problem in every case.

Behavior charts are the second line of defense if your child doesn't respond to explanations. Before you begin using behavior charts, please review chapter 12.

Here are some recommendations for items on a behavior chart to tackle school behaviors:

- Stay in your seat during class.
- Do what the teachers ask the first time they ask.
- Raise your hand and wait to be called on before you speak.
- Use kind words and kind actions toward teachers and students.

Once you set up the behavior chart and reward system, explain to your child how they work. Make sure your child understands that you plan to contact the teachers about their conduct to verify that they successfully completed the behaviors.

Email the teachers who were complaining to explain how you will be working on managing your child's school conduct. Please include the behavior chart and ask if any other desired behaviors need to be added. Ask the teachers for daily feedback until the undesirable behaviors disappear.

A few teachers may balk at the request because they're busy, but most are grateful that you are trying to help and are happy to work with you.

Often, school behaviors are not the only problem. Many children present problem behaviors at home.

TWENTY-ONE

Homework Wars

Your child is always looking for ways to avoid doing homework. You're worried and fed up with the constant strife to make sure it gets done. To assess the problem, you need more information before looking for the cause or a remedy. Here are some questions to ask yourself.

Was homework an ongoing problem from the start of this school year, or did it only begin a few months ago? The answer gives you a clue as to whether your child is stuck because of learning issues, personality style, or a breakdown in your relationship.

Homework wars are draining. You and the kids are worn out from school and work and would love nothing better than to sit and relax. Children who struggle with schoolwork and come home tired need a break. Sitting down to do homework right away is overwhelming to them. However, homework has to be completed and checked, and dinner has to be cooked.

Here are some common reasons for refusing to complete assignments and how to spot them.

Reasons for Homework Issues or Outright Refusal

- Perfectionism
- Power struggles
- Anger at parents
- Pressure to excel
- Learning disabilities
- Slow processing speed
- Assignments that are too hard

How to Spot Homework Refusal

- Procrastination
- Pitching a tantrum over doing homework
- Sitting with the homework and staring into space
- Running off and refusing to sit and do homework
- Saying it's completed and turned in when it's not (lying)
- Delaying homework until late at night and then asking for help

How to Determine What Is Going On

If refusal has been an ongoing problem, the assignments may be too hard, or your child's homework schedule needs to be modified.

Recommendation

You can use the following as an example of a conversation you can have if the refusal issue cropped up more recently.

You: "I can tell you don't like doing homework. You used to do it before. Is something wrong?"

Sam: "No, nothing's wrong. I just don't want to do it."

You: "Sometimes kids stop doing homework because they're mad at their teacher or their parents."

Sam: Sam looks up but says nothing.

You: "Sometimes the homework is too hard, but the parents aren't good at helping."

Sam: "Yes, it's hard."

You: "Does the teacher have tutoring hours?"

Sam: "I hate my teacher. She's dumb."

You: "Would you like an outside tutor to help you?"

Sam: "I dunno."

You: "Can we try?"

Sam: "OK."

If the conversation goes nowhere, contact the teacher to find out if Sam needs assistance with classwork. The teacher's input will help you determine whether he's struggling with schoolwork or having a power struggle with you or with his teacher.

What to Do if the Homework Assignments Are Too Hard

If your child has learning disabilities or a slow thought-processing speed, the problems will show up at school, not just at home. You can email their teachers to ask if they see the same issues.

Request a school psychological assessment if one has not been performed. Some children are not identified early because they are quiet and don't cause problems.

Often, children who are shy at school feel free to express themselves at home—and do they ever!

Yet the homework must be done *tonight* and for the next several years of school.

Here are some tips on how you can help:

- Set a schedule for homework time and stick to the plan, even if the child lives in two households.

- Break the homework into ten-minute or twenty-minute chunks with five-minute breaks in between. The breaks include drinking water, jumping jacks, or other in-place exercises—*no TV or electronics during the breaks.*

- Tell your child they can work longer to solve problems or write their thoughts down. You can test how many minutes they can tolerate before a break and change the time after discussing such a change with them.

- *No one watches TV or uses electronics while your child is busy with homework*—not even the adults in the house. The younger siblings can do their own "homework" by sitting down to color.

- Be encouraging. You are the cheerleader in this process.

- Make sure your child does their work. Regardless of your tiredness, avoid being tempted to do the work for them. Such actions show a lack of faith and respect for your child's abilities. Doing their homework for them sets up an expectation that you will always do their work for them.

Maybe It's a Time Management Issue

Some children have slow processing speed plus time management issues, which makes everything take longer. Slow processing looks like procrastination, but it's not. Chapter 34 includes detailed information about these types of problems, as well as tips on how to help as a parent.

Delaying doing homework can also be a result of anger.

Example of Anger at Parents

If homework refusal is a new behavior for your child or has become more frequent, the root cause can be anger at you, the parent. At some point, you may have "promised" some reward for completing all the homework but failed to keep the promise. Such a misunderstanding can be based on an old conversation.

For example, you are preoccupied with work concerns when your daughter approaches you.

Amy: "If I do all my homework from now until the end of the year, can I get a nose ring?"

You: "Uh-huh."

At the start of summer vacation:

Amy: "Can we go get the nose ring this weekend?"

You: "Absolutely not! I told you before. No face or belly piercings."

Amy: "But you promised!"

You: "I did no such thing!"

The first conversation made Amy believe the two of you had a deal. In her eyes, you are not keeping your part of the bargain. Amy then decides to punish you and stops doing her homework. She feels betrayed and knows you consider homework and grades important. Amy is unaware she is hurting herself through her actions. Her only thought is revenge.

If you suspect your child may be refusing to do homework to spite or punish you, discuss your suspicion with them.

You: "Are you skipping your homework to show me you're angry with me?"

Amy: "I just don't want to do homework."

You: "Sometimes kids get mad at their parents about something, and if the parents consider homework and grades important, the kids stop doing homework. Are you angry with me about something?"

Amy: "I think homework is stupid and a waste of time."

You: "I thought so too, but I did my homework because school was my job as a kid. If you're angry with me about something and don't tell me, then I can't fix it."

Amy: "It's about the nose ring. You promised!"

Hear Amy out. Find out when you made such a promise. Explain that you weren't listening and offer to put all future promises in writing so that there is no confusion. Also, offer a different reward for the past good homework performance.

Example of a Power Struggle

Your Tim is very forceful and determined, just like you. He wages many battles with you, but you consider homework important.

Here is a typical after-school conversation:

You: "Tim, what homework do you have today?"

Tim: "I finished it at school."

You: "Let me see it. I'll check it over."

Tim: "It doesn't need to be checked. I know what I'm doing!"

You: "I still want to see the work."

Tim: "You don't trust me!"

You: "Bring your school laptop here. I have to get dinner started."

Tim: "I have to go to the bathroom."

Tim disappears until dinner is served.

Setting up a behavior chart is the easiest way to combat the situation. If what you're seeing is a rebellion, the behavior will disappear. Your child will be doing the homework for the rewards, not because you said so. If the problem includes a knowledge gap, your child will still want the rewards and so will ask for help with the work. Rebellion and learning problems can coexist.

On the behavior chart, list the desired behaviors as follows:

1. Complete assigned homework.
2. Let parents check homework before you submit it.
3. Correct any mistakes.
4. Submit homework.

Pick a motivator for completed homework. Money works with some kids, and video-game time works with others. Your child may have a different motivator. Make that their reward.

Chapter 12 is devoted to setting up behavior charts; please refer to it for further instructions.

Perfectionism

Perfectionism generates a lot of anxiety, which can lead to procrastination or excessive time spent on each assignment. It's impossible to do the homework perfectly, but your child tries. She rewrites things, erases, and redraws until it's time to sleep, but it turns out she worked on only one assignment.

Be kind and gentle. Teach her to limit her time on certain parts of the homework.

Teach her to finish all the tasks first and then go back and review. You may have to sit with her and praise what she produces. Perhaps the praise will be enough to stop her from trying to redo everything. Just stopping her from redoing the work will create massive anxiety. Please refer to chapter 31 to learn how to help her be less anxious.

Whether the issue is procrastination or overthinking, teaching your children time management helps.

Another big issue in many homes is the morning routine.

TWENTY-TWO

Morning Routines

Morning routines are a frequent battleground for school-age kids. The parents buzz around trying to prepare for work and expect the kids to get themselves ready. Some do, but others engage in stalling, arguing over clothes, watching TV, or fighting with siblings. In some households, these behaviors become a pattern.

Behavior charts are a perfect tool for these situations. But behavior charts take time.

Here is a method to break up the old pattern that you and your children created.

To break up the pattern, you must pretend you're not rushed. I recommend getting up earlier to avoid becoming stressed out.

Here are some common scenarios.

Example of Delaying Getting Up

Usually, you pop into Sue's bedroom, wake her up, and go downstairs to prepare breakfast. This time, Sue pulls the covers over her head and remains in bed.

You: "Sue, good morning! It's time to get up!"
Sue: Sue slides deeper under the covers. "I'm sleepy."

You: "What did you decide to wear today?"
       You're not following a familiar pattern of leaving the room.
Sue: "Huh?"
You: "The weatherman says it's going to be warm today. Will you wear pants or shorts?"
Sue: "I don't know."
You: "Do you want me to pick out your clothes?"
Sue: Sue jumps out of bed. "No!"
You: You sit down on Sue's bed. "OK."
Sue: "I have to brush my teeth first."
You: "Good idea. What do you want for breakfast?"
       Sue tried to get you into a familiar pattern, but you skirted around it.
Sue: "Cheerios."
You: "Coming right up!"

Recommendation

To break up the pattern, change how you respond to the original "I'm sleepy" comment. Don't leave the room to return later for an argument. Stand your ground until your child is well into her getting-ready-for-school routine.

Example of Arguing over Clothes

You: "Mia, it's too cold for shorts."
Mia: "No, it's not."
You: "The weather report said it will be cold outside."
Mia: "I don't have any pants that go with this shirt!"
You: "This shirt is too thin to wear in this weather. Please pick another."
Mia: Mia slams around in her closet and chest of drawers. "Are you going to stand there while I get dressed?"
You: "Yes. It'll save time so that you don't have to change your clothes before we leave."

142

Recommendation

If your child is particular about clothes and takes a long time to pick an outfit and get dressed, help her develop a new habit of selecting clothes the evening before. Such a schedule adjustment shows that you respect your child's concern with wardrobe, and it teaches her to plan and prepare.

Example of Being Engrossed in Electronics Instead of Getting Ready

Everyone is having breakfast except for Don, who is watching TV in his pajamas.

Recommendation

Establish a rule of no TV or other electronics before everyone is ready to leave. That means no background TV or phones for anyone in the family. Once the rule is in place, you can have the following conversation with your son:

You: "Remember what I told you, Don. If you're not dressed and haven't eaten breakfast before it's time to leave, you're going to school in your pajamas and without breakfast."

Don: "Huh?"

You: Turn off the TV. Put Don's face in your hands, look him in the eye, and repeat, "Remember what I told you, Don. If you're not dressed and haven't eaten breakfast before it's time to leave, you're going to school in your pajamas and without breakfast."

Don: "OK. I'm going."

If Don decides to call your bluff about taking him to school in his pajamas, grab his shoes and clothes and usher him into the car in his pajamas and without breakfast. He can change his clothes in the car and skip breakfast.

Example of Fighting and Arguing with Siblings

Some kids like to get everyone riled up in the morning and annoy a sibling until a fight erupts. You can make a general announcement that the fighting stops now, or everyone loses access to electronics for a week, no matter who started the fight.

Recommendation

Is fighting a frequent scenario at your house? You can handle this behavior by creating a special behavior chart that involves all the kids. The reward has to be something they all love. "If you go a week without a single fight or loud argument, each of you will get movie theater tickets. If you only fight once during the week, you get nothing. It has to be seven days of no fighting or arguing."

Morning routines exist in all families. If you don't like the pattern your family has fallen into, break it up and rearrange it using the examples presented in this chapter.

Many parents struggle with their kids during evening routines when it's time to wind down and sleep.

TWENTY-THREE

Bedtime Battles

Bedtime is a frequent battleground with toddlers, so you're not alone.

Unfortunately, the timing couldn't be worse. You're tired from a day of work, getting everyone fed, and cleaning up. The last thing you need is a prolonged struggle around bath time or bedtime. You're dreaming of going to bed to read a little or watch TV. Instead, you're confronted with your child, who seems determined not to go to bed and not to allow you to rest.

Let's begin with the possible causes of such behaviors before we move on to ways of managing them.

Triggers for Bedtime Battles

There are four possible triggers for bedtime battles:

1. The child is anxious about something.
2. The child is not tired and needs to dissipate extra energy to relax.
3. You are gone until late evening, and your child wants to extend their special time with you.
4. The child likes to engage in power struggles.

Instead of everyone calming down and preparing for a restful night, you and your child become locked in a battle.

We need to understand what is causing the behaviors. Let's begin with the most sensitive cause.

Your Anxious Child

Your child may have been content with the old bedtime routine until they became anxious about something. Fearfulness or worrying can lead to delaying going to bed or, once in bed, refusing to let you leave the room until they fall asleep.

Sources of anxiety can include the following:

- Nightmares
- Shadows in the room
- Strange sounds outside or inside
- A belief in ghosts or monsters under the bed or in the closet
- The perception of strangers outside the window trying to get in

Your child is visibly frightened, shaking, crying, and clingy.

Recommendation

You realize your child is nervous about something or even terrified. You may have asked what scares her. Sometimes she can tell you, sometimes not. She may not have the words for her fears yet.

Fearfulness is not a case for tough love.

One way of working with fear is storytelling. You can go to the local library and ask for books about bedtime fears for toddlers or look online for books on the subject. I prefer telling my own stories. If your toddler is a boy, tell a story about a boy. If she is a girl, make the story about a girl. Add small details about your child's hair or personality so that they can identify with the character.

Here is a story example:

Suzie is a beautiful little girl with short brown hair and bangs. She has a mommy who loves her very much. Suzie is lucky to have a bedroom with her own bed. But she doesn't feel lucky. She feels very alone and scared when everyone kisses her good night and leaves.

Suzie's mommy doesn't understand why she is scared, and Suzie can't find the words to tell her why. But she sees shadows in the room. When the wind blows the big tree outside, the shadows move. Some shadows look like people, and some look like monsters.

When it's dark outside and she can't see the shadows, Suzie thinks the monsters are hiding in her closet or under the bed. She is afraid to go to the bathroom at night because she's worried one of them might grab her and take her far away from her mommy.

Suzie is so scared she starts crying and shaking when her mommy tries to tuck her in to go to sleep. She grabs her mommy around the neck and won't let go. Mommy asks her, "Are you scared?" Suzie nods. Mommy says, "I'll stay with you until you fall asleep." Suzie is happy. Mommy rubs her feet and strokes her hair until Suzie falls asleep.

If you don't like to make up stories, you can read books about the fear of darkness and being alone so that your child can learn that all kids and animals are scared of being alone. Teach your child words such as *darkness, monsters, ghosts,* and *shadows* so that she can tell you what is scaring her.

If your child is afraid of shadows, show her how shadows are created in the sunlight, on the sidewalk, and in her room at night. Turn the light off in her room and use a light source to make hand shadow puppets on the wall. If you are unfamiliar with shadow puppets, use Google to find many examples.

If your child fears the dark, you can leave a low light on in the room or give her a flashlight she can turn on herself.

You can also play a hide-and-seek game in a dark room with your child. Cover the window in a small room to make it pitch-black. You move away from your child and say, "I'm here. Come and get me!" Make sure your child can find you easily. Keep calling out so that she knows you're there. Then switch roles. Your child will move away from you and say, "I'm here!" You pretend you can't find her, move away from her, and keep calling, "Where are you?"

The intent is to extend the game in the dark and make it fun so that your child feels successful. The fun and sense of achievement for successfully playing hide-and-seek in the dark help eliminate the fear.

If your child fears being carried off in the middle of the night by an intruder, you can show her how the window locks so that no one can get in from the outside.

Fears are tough to conquer, but these methods will help.

But perhaps you have a child with too much energy at bedtime.

Your Energetic Child

Some children have a natural abundance of energy and have difficulty settling into a relaxed state. In the hyperalert state, you can understand why they resist going to bed and get stuck lying there for hours without being able to fall asleep.

An energetic child is easy to spot. They attempt to engage you in chasing games and bounce on the couch or the bed when everyone else is winding down.

Staying up as a result of energy overload may look like a power struggle, but it's not.

Recommendation

The reason your child has too much energy at bedtime is unimportant. No matter the cause of it, the remedy is the same. Create activities and games to dissipate the energy so that they're tired before bedtime. Invent games involving a lot of running, such as races up and down the stairs. You stay put with a timer. Have your child race up and down the street to a specific tree and back. Time your child with each run and challenge them to beat their record. If you're in a home without stairs, your child can do sit-ups, push-ups, or jumping jacks, or they can jump on and off the couch while you sit back and do the counting.

Staying up as a result of energy overload may look like a power struggle, but it's not. Strong-minded toddlers who engage in power struggles are in a class of their own.

Your Clingy Child

You may work long hours that keep you away from home. Then, when you're home, your child tries to hang on to you, even if the behavior leads to getting in trouble. Attention is important to young kids.

Power Struggles

Delaying the bedtime routine or taking too long getting out of the tub or shower is your bossy child's version of a power struggle. Instead of calming down and preparing for a restful night, you and your child become locked in a battle of wills. Kids often go through stages as they attempt to assert themselves and advocate for what they prefer. Your child has their sights on controlling their nighttime routine.

You don't want to spend your evenings in strife, no matter the cause of the behavior.

You want solutions.

Recommendation

It takes two to make a conflict. If you let your child have their way at bedtime, there will be no conflict, but there will be no bedtime either. Find a way around the power struggle so that your child can do what you want them to, but not because you said so.

Young children thrive on structure. They feel calm and are most cooperative when they know what will happen next and what will happen after that.

Create a nighttime routine schedule for your little rebel. Such a schedule has to be in pictures. If your child resists doing the next thing in the routine, you can show him the schedule. If he still resists, you can use the following technique:

You: "Sam, we're done with dinner. Do you remember what comes next?"

Sam: "Watch cartoon."

You: "That's right! You remember! What comes after the cartoon?"

Sam: "Brush teeth."

You: "That's right!"

After your child has watched cartoons for the allowed amount of time, move on to the next step.

You: "Oh good. You're done watching the cartoon. What comes next?"

Sam: "Brush teeth."

You: "And after that?"

Sam: "Bath!"

You: "That's right. I'll race you to the bathroom."

While he is brushing his teeth, count the strokes of the toothbrush. The distraction of counting will help your child forget about protesting.

You: "Is it time to run the water for the bath?"

Sam: "Yes."

You: "Brushing is all done. What comes next?"

Sam: "Bath!"

You: "That's right, and after that?"

Sam: "PJs!"

You: "That's right!"

Use the same conversational rhythm for the rest of your routine. You may have noticed you used this conversation style to give Sam the power. He feels like he's directing the activity.

We covered four possible sources of nighttime battles. You can copy my methods or create approaches better suited to the situation and your child's personality.

The Triggers for Bedtime Battles Are Not Mutually Exclusive

Your child can have multiple reasons for putting off going to sleep. They can be in a power struggle with you and have too much energy. They can be anxious and miss the absent parent. Any combination is possible. If your child experiences multiple reasons for disturbed nighttime routines, you can combine all the tools provided in the various chapters to handle your unique situation.

As we'll discuss in the next chapter, the children who get into power struggles at home often take the battle to the store.

TWENTY-FOUR

Shopping with Three Kids

Some parents avoid taking their kids shopping because they cause an uproar. Displays of unruly, loud, and demanding behaviors cause the parents to become stressed, angry, and embarrassed. Children who usually behave well might pick the store as the stage for their horrible-kids act.

Example of Shopping with Three Kids

On the way to the store, you can feel yourself tensing up in the car.

You: "When we get to the store, I want you to be on your best behavior."
There are three kids in the car. Only nine-year-old Kim responds.
Kim: "Yes, Mom."
At the store, you put Dean, the youngest, in the shopping cart seat and try to get Tom, the five-year-old, into the cart.
Tom: "I want to walk!"

You: "OK, but you have to hold on to the cart. Now where is my shopping list?"

You left your shopping list at home but think you can remember everything. The little procession starts peacefully and stops in the cereal aisle.

Tom: "I want the Lucky Charms cereal!" Tom runs, grabs the cereal, and throws it into the basket.

You: "No. That has too much sugar in it. Let's get Cheerios. Kim, can you get the Cheerios and put the Lucky Charms back?"

Kim: "OK."

Tom: "I want Lucky Charms!"

You: "Let's get the milk."

You wheel the cart to the dairy section. Tom stays behind.

You: "Kim, can you please get your brother?"

Kim: "OK."

You select the milk and scan the egg prices. Dean grabs a carton of eggs, which falls out of his little hands. In the background, you can hear Tom wailing, "I want Lucky Charms!" His sister is trying to calm him down as she drags him away from the cereal aisle. Once Tom spots that his brother has smashed the eggs, he forgets about the cereal.

Tom: "Did Dean break the eggs?"

You: "Yes. It was an accident."

Tom: "Are you going to punish him?"

You: "Not right now. He's little. Dean, no grabbing!"

Now everyone is agitated, but you have only three items in the shopping cart. Similar scenes occur in the produce department and in the bread section. Finally, you make it to the checkout stand.

Tom: "I want this candy." Tom grabs at the candy.

You: "No candy. I told you in the car, no candy."

Tom keeps grabbing at the candy and throws some in the cart. Dean is busy trying to reach the things behind him to put on the conveyor belt. He tries to be helpful but drops the loaf of bread on the floor. Kim is trying to fish the candy out of the cart, and you are busy loading things on the conveyor belt as quickly as possible.

Tom: *"I want candy! I want candy! I want candy!"*

Kim: *"Shh.* Everyone is staring at us."

Let's look at the kids' perspective before we discuss how to manage the behavior.

Why Do Kids Behave This Way at the Store?

Let's look at the shopping experience from a child's perspective. You get into the store, and all the adults ignore you. Your mom is busy scanning the shelves for what she came to buy. All the other adults are either staring at the displays or touching things. No one is paying attention to you, and you're not allowed to touch anything. Shopping is boring. You get shut down when you try to pick something you want.

How to Improve the Shopping Experience

Your goal is to engage the kids in the process so that they can feel your attention and approval. Being involved in shopping keeps them from becoming bored. Here is a list of tips:

- Make a shopping list together with the kids.
- Have an older child make the list.
- If you have two readers, the other can be the reader of the list at the store.
- The child who can walk can be in charge of finding the items on your list.
- You follow with the shopping cart, make suggestions if they falter, and give praise.
- Use the time at the store to teach new words, quantities, and concepts.
- At home, call Dad or Grandma to recap all the things the kids did to help.

What if the System Does Not Work?

This system may not be enough for a child like Tom. If your child likes to engage in power struggles or is restless to the point of poor self-control, you may have to use behavior charts to motivate them to be more cooperative at the store.

The behavior chart can include whatever behaviors you want to see at the store. Here are some examples:

- Do what I ask the first time I ask.
- Hold on to the cart.
- Stay with the cart.
- Stay in the seat.
- Hold the items with both hands.

For best results, please study chapter 12 on behavior charts. Your behavior chart must be set up and followed in a specific way; otherwise, the method won't work.

Older kids don't misbehave in stores. Instead, if they want to get out of doing something, they will engage you in an endless debate to avoid doing what you asked.

TWENTY-FIVE

Debating, Interrupting, and Correcting

Preteens use the debating strategy. Debating is a form of power struggle disguised as a "logical" discussion. From the child's perspective, the main goal is to distract you from the subject and confuse you so that they can either get you off their back or get a yes following some requests.

Example of Debating

Ann has always questioned every request. Here is a typical conversation between the two of you:

You: "Ann, clean your room before you leave the house today."
Ann: "There's no time. I'm late already."
You: "Late for what?"
Ann: "My friends and I are going to basketball practice."
You: "You don't have practice today."
Ann: "We decided to go to the gym and practice on our own."
You: "What gym are you going to?"

Ann: "The usual."

You: "Which is?"

Ann: "Oh, Mom!"

Now you're worried that you're not getting the whole scoop and that they're not really going to a gym. You almost forgot about your initial request to clean the room.

You: "I can take you there after you clean your room."

Ann: "Oh, Mom! We were going to go with Leanne's mom."

You: "I don't know Leanne."

Ann: "Oh, Mom."

What follows is a debate about how she needs to keep a promise. Everyone forgets about cleaning the room.

Recommendation

To get around Ann's dodging, you can try the following:

You: "Ann, clean your room before you leave the house today."

Ann: "There's no time. I'm late already."

You: "Your room needs cleaning now."

Ann: "But my friends are waiting for me!"

You: "Your room needs cleaning now. It's Saturday morning. The rule is not to leave the house until your room is clean."

Ann: "But I'll miss practice!"

You: "Clean your room first. I'll explain to the coach."

Ann: "But blah, blah, blah..."

You: "Clean your room first."

Ann: "But blah, blah, blah..."

You: "Clean your room first."

Recommendation

If establishing a habit of keeping a clean room is important to you as a parent, you might set a day when you know your kids have free time and are not interrupted by sports or other essential activities. Make a rule that Saturday, for example, is the day for your child to clean their room before they leave the house. Get cooperation with behavior charts to establish a habit of cleaning the room once a week.

Example of Interrupting

Dad is working from home. He's on a Zoom call, and Tom knows not to interrupt him.

Tom: Tom bursts into Dad's home office. "Here's your mail!"
Dad waves him away. Tom goes to the kitchen, where Mom is talking to the electrician.

Tom: "I gave Dad his mail."

You: "Not now, Tom."

Tom: Tom listens to the conversation with the electrician for thirty seconds. "When is dinner? I'm hungry."

Recommendation

The repetitive interrupting of conversations is an attention-getting device. A persistent child can benefit from an intervention with a behavior chart. A more immediate intervention is recognizing the interruption as a ploy for attention. Dad cannot do anything differently, but Mom can include Tom in the conversation with the electrician. She can introduce Tom by name and mention that he's a great help to her. Mom might ask Tom how long it has been since the light stopped working.

Example of Correcting

Sue has failed to follow her mom's instructions to clean her room.

You: "Sue, I asked you to clean your room two times today."

Sue: "No. You only asked me one time."

You: "I asked you this morning before you went to school and when you got back."

Sue: "No, you didn't ask me this morning. You told me."

You: "I'm telling you again. Go to your room now and start picking things up."

You stand at the doorway to Sue's room.

Sue: "OK, but my room doesn't need picking up."

You: "What are you talking about? There's stuff all over the floor. You can't see the carpet."

Sue: Sue points to a clear corner of the room. "You can see the carpet over there."

Recommendation

In the following example, Sue tries to control the situation by passively avoiding, deflecting, and correcting. Passive avoidance responds to intervention with a behavior chart. For a more immediate intervention, try steering the conversation.

You: "Sue, I asked you to clean your room two times today."

Sue: "No. You only asked me one time."

You: "It's time to get started. Let's go."

Sue: "It's not even messy."

You stand at the doorway to Sue's room.

You: "Which corner do you pick for a starting point?"

Choosing the corner to begin cleaning avoids the arguments and gives Sue some control over the situation because she gets to decide on a starting point.

Debating, interrupting, and correcting are relatively easy to manage, but manipulation on the part of your child is more challenging.

TWENTY-SIX

Manipulation

By eighteen months, every self-respecting baby can tell who in the family is the easy touch. As children get older, they learn to manipulate. Their favorite technique is the game of "lets you and him fight" (and I'll slip away and do what I want). If you fall for this trick, you may have a hard time controlling the situation, and your family life will be in constant uproar.

Preteens are exceptionally skilled at the game of "lets you and him fight."

Your kids want to go somewhere with their friends, and you don't want them to. They go to the other, more permissive adult and get a yes. Then you argue with the other adult, and the kids go off to play video games.

If this is how your child manipulates you, I recommend you have the following conversation with them:

You: "I will discuss it with your father, and we will let you know."

Kid: "But they need to have the answer now!"

You: "If it has to be right now, then the answer is no."

Such responses let your child know that manipulations won't work—even if they've worked for the past eight years. The behavior stops once the child knows this is a new regime. As with all behaviors that you're trying to end, you get a spike in the old behavior as the child tries to get you back into your old groove. When your child realizes the method no longer works, the manipulation stops.

In general, it's a good idea to discuss the behaviors you see and the requests with all the adults in the immediate family so that you can decide on a single course of action. If you cannot reach an agreement, the best tip I can give you is to make the strictest decision.

Your child will fume, but they will be glad to have a clear direction so that they can tell their friends, "No go. My parents are really strict," or "My parents are such jerks. I can't go."

If you think you are depriving your child and ruining their friendships, be aware that you never get the whole story. They may be subjected to peer pressure and do not really want to participate, so you're just giving them an easy out.

You will find the strict approach helpful when your child becomes a teenager.

TWENTY-SEVEN

Children of Divorce

You feel relieved.

The divorce is final.

But the stress is just beginning for the kids.

No matter what arrangement you or the courts choose, it complicates their life. Your child's perspective is different.

Young Children Don't Understand Divorce

You and your spouse split up, and your child thinks you don't want to be with them. They worry they did something wrong, which made one of you leave. Such a reaction is more likely if you argue about the child within their earshot.

They think you're leaving them, not your ex.

Kids Think Their Parents Are Omnipotent

If there were many arguments before the divorce to the point that your child couldn't sleep or was worried for everyone's safety, they might feel relieved that the fighting has stopped.

On the other hand, if you've kept your conflict hidden, your child might be resentful that you didn't fix the problem to keep things stable and together for them. The resentment can be expressed in tone of voice, lack of eye contact, and disobedience.

Explaining that it wasn't your fault is futile.

Shared Custody

One of you has the kids during the week, and the other has them on weekends, with Wednesday night at the weekend parent's house. Think of the logistics. They must remember their clothes, homework, and whatever they need for school on Thursday, Monday, or the weekend.

The kids can keep the same friends if you live in the same area. But if one of you moves farther away, the weekend friends have to be different from the weekday friends.

How would you like to keep that kind of routine?

Parents' New Partners

You're happy because you found a new partner. You hope your child and partner bond with each other. From your child's point of view, they gained a parent. Every adult has their own set of expectations and way of parenting. Your ex may also find a new partner. Now your child has four parents to please, respect, or pretend to respect. Four people telling a child what to do!

How would you like to have four bosses?

Parents Vying to Be the Favorite

Some parents try to get their child to pick them as their favorite. Such contests can involve bribing or emotional manipulation by the parents. The child reacts with confusion, disgust, misbehavior, or manipulation. Such maneuvering stresses your child.

Expressing Frustration with Your Ex in Front of Your Child

Parents who wanted full custody but didn't get it are the most prone to complaining about the ex in front of their child. They feel wronged and are determined to fix the wrong by reopening the fight for full custody.

Young children suffer the most because they are helpless in the situation. Moving between parental homes is stressful, and they cry during parent exchanges. The parents take this behavior as a sign they love the other parent better when, in fact, they are just responding to the manipulation of the parent who wanted full custody.

The tug-of-war over the kids leads to acting out at home and at school.

Please stop talking to your child about your ex's faults because your child is part of you and part of your ex. Is your child half-bad? Do you want your child to think he's half-bad and you don't love him because he acts or looks like the other parent?

Your ex must have had some good qualities. If you must talk about your ex, focus on those.

Trying to Control How Your Ex Parents Your Child

You've never approved of your ex's parenting style. Now you pump your child about what happens at the ex's house. You send lengthy emails with instructions on how to work with your child. You may even go to therapy to try to get the therapist to talk your ex into changing their ways.

Trust your child to do the right thing. It's OK for your child to experience different parenting styles. They will likely grow up to have several bosses, all of whom will have different expectations.

Relax. Breathe.

Your Preteen Chooses to Live with Your Ex

Please don't take their decision to move in with the other parent personally.

Your preteen wants to pick a single location. They are in their selfish stage and choose a household and a neighborhood that best suits them. They're closer to their friends than you, and their decision is based on whom they wish to spend time with.

Maintain contact with your child. Remember, soon they will be adults. If you've been good to them, they will return to you.

Be Considerate of Your Child's Situation

You have much on your plate. Setting up a single-parent household, working, and shuttling the kids back and forth is a lot. Remember, the kids didn't ask for this arrangement.

- Be considerate.
- Make a list for them to follow.
- Be sympathetic when they complain about being uprooted.
- Keep the same schedule for after-school activities in both homes.
- Acknowledge feelings of anger, worry, grief, and abandonment.
- Let your child talk. Avoid interrupting with excuses or impatience.
- Help them remember their stuff when they stay with the other parent.
- Acknowledge the sadness of the little ones, and remind them they can see the other parent soon.
- If your child shows qualities you admired in your ex, say, "You did this great, just like your mom/dad."
- Avoid saying, "You're just like your father/mother" when the child messes up.
- Try to parent cooperatively with your ex.

Whether you're single or married, parenting becomes incrementally trickier until your child reaches the preteen stage. There's a shift from you being their whole world to peers becoming their primary people to please and impress. Suddenly, you're on the outside looking in.

TWENTY-EIGHT

The Preteen Years

You notice your child is more aware of other people, especially peers. Friendships are valued more than family. Parents feel their child slipping away and separating as their bonds with friends strengthen. Suddenly, what you think matters less than what their friends think.

Secure in the knowledge that they have a special place in their family, a child seeks their place among peers. Cliques begin to form. Peer pressure is introduced and threatens the values you taught them. Belonging to a group becomes important. Lack of peer acceptance can become a problem.

Your child, who never cared what they wore as long as it was comfortable, becomes style conscious. When you see them with their friends, their hair and clothes all look alike. Your child sports new styles, attitudes, and mannerisms. Preteens compare themselves to peers and seek their approval. For some, it's the beginning of problems with body image. Others may develop eating disorders.

Hugging them in public becomes taboo.

Although their attention span increases, their interest in doing schoolwork takes a nosedive. Some kids will tell you point-blank they go to school to socialize, not to learn.

It's a time of all-or-nothing thinking. Actions are either right or wrong. Clothes and hairstyles are either right or wrong. Events in their lives are either fantastic or terrible. You see overreactions to what was said or done fueled by their black-and-white thinking and hormones.

Hormones and Puberty

Hormone changes are not uniform for all kids of the same age. Some kids' bodies change early, and some are delayed. The uneven development leads to more comparisons and embarrassment. You may notice your child attempting to hide their developing body with oversize clothing. They seek more privacy when bathing and dressing.

Some kids are concerned about maturing too fast, and others worry about not maturing fast enough. Some kids don't want the changes at all. They are shocked by the physical changes and want them to stop. They don't want to mature into the next stage, or they find the changes foreign and disturbing. Such reactions cause psychological problems as the kids question their identities. Being unable to control what is happening to them can be very distressing.

The hormone changes can lead to mood swings and problems with decision-making.

The Decision-Making Part of the Preteen Brain Is Still Under Construction

Brain development continues into the midtwenties. Preteens do not yet have good judgment but are now less willing to listen to parents. As a precaution, ensure that your child's friends are the type less likely to have wild ideas about exciting activities. Get to know their friends. Make it easy and inviting for their friends to come over and hang out.

Some preteens are curious, kind, and silly. They are interested in the world around them and want to learn as much as possible. They read, watch informational shows, and enjoy group activities with peers where they can improve themselves. These activities include sports, choir, band, chess, and electronics clubs.

Others are self-absorbed, moody, and disrespectful. Their curiosity is limited to things you disapprove of. Preteens believe their emotions and thoughts are different from those of everyone else. You are told, "You don't understand!" They question authority, test limits, and push boundaries. Your child feels invincible, which causes you to worry. You find yourself telling them to make good choices.

For some, it's a time of firsts, such as a crush or pretend crush to fit in—plus first attempts at smoking, vaping, drinking, marijuana, or pills.

Your preteen needs to develop self-discipline. They won't learn self-monitoring if you impose discipline on them with overly strict limits.

Harness Curiosity and Set Limits

With preteens, their decision-making does not keep pace with their appetite for novelty and adventure. You have to set limits and find ways to engage them in stimulating after-school and weekend activities that satisfy their need for novelty, excitement, and physical achievement.

Limit setting can include curfews and finishing schoolwork and chores before doing fun things.

You spend your time chauffeuring them to activities, watching them in sports, listening to them practice musical instruments, or watching them create art. If you haven't visited museums before, this is a good time to start. Take them to parks, to different parts of town, to a wild nature spot, on a fishing trip, to volunteer activities, or on walks. Because their interests fluctuate, you have to put up with starting and stopping different sports and musical instruments.

Often, their interest in a sport depends on what their friends are involved in. That's fine, as long as they are engaged. Use their need to be with their friends when attempting to get them to do something that sounds boring. Tell them they can bring a friend along. More time spent with you means less exposure to peer pressure.

Ask your preteen to find activities they like. Nowadays, finding things to do in your area is easy. All you have to do is ask Google or some other app. Your child can do that. If they take the lead, they will be more interested in going there. Take them if you can afford it. Bring one of their friends along.

If you don't do something to engage their interest and curiosity, they may spend excessive time on social media or computer games, which has its own set of risks.

PART 4

Concerning Situations That May Require Professional Intervention

TWENTY-NINE

Anger

Some children display anger from a very young age. Sometimes anger is genetic, as evidenced by one of the parent's short fuses. If neither of the parents' tempers flare up quickly, you may find an aunt, an uncle, or a grandparent whose temper does.

Others learn angry reactions from family members, other kids, or videos. Angry reactions can become a habit, so it's important to teach your child better ways of handling emotions than yelling, kicking, scratching, biting, or hitting.

Certain conditions trigger anger:

- Disappointment or betrayal
- Feeling powerless
- Feeling frustrated
- Feeling guilty
- Dwelling on things that incite anger
- Old habits/patterns with certain people
- Neurological excitation in the form of excess energy
- Hypoglycemia (low blood sugar)
- Lead poisoning
- Being under the influence of drugs (uppers) or alcohol
- Coming off drugs
- Steroid use

Only the first few items apply to young children, but they all apply to teens and adults. Anger is an emotion, and all emotions are healthy in moderation. But if your child reacts with anger so often that others shun them and you have trouble managing them, it's time to intervene.

Anger Is Excess Energy

Anger and excess energy go together. Anger causes body excitation, which turns into excess energy. On the other hand, excess energy can quickly turn to anger. In children, such anger is displayed by yelling, tantrums, hitting, throwing, and biting. As an adult, you can decide to use the anger energy to make positive changes in your life, or you can use your anger to self-destruct and destroy others. Young children have to be taught how to manage their angry feelings.

Acknowledging Feelings

Joanna Faber and Julie King wrote a book, *How to Talk So Little Kids Will Listen* (2017). The basic premise is that to resolve a young child's upset feelings, the caretakers must acknowledge both the feelings and the situation that caused them. Then the adults can share their feelings and move on to problem-solving. Recognizing a child's feelings is often enough to calm them when they are upset or angry.

But what if that doesn't work? You can't problem-solve with a raging child. First you have to tone down the anger.

How to Stop Your Child's Anger Once It's Here

Slow breathing, exercise, thought stopping, and thought replacement are the primary methods for controlling a child's angry feelings and making them disappear. When the level of anger is down, you can discuss triggers.

Calming an Angry Child on Your Lap

Invite your child to sit on your lap to calm down, as shown in the picture. Intertwine your fingers with your child's. Breathe slowly to pass the calm energy to your child. Rock back and forth at your child's breathing speed. Then slow the rocking to see if your child slows their breathing. Stay in this position and rock until you feel your child's body relax.

Example of Teaching Slow and Even Breathing

You have observed your five-year-old Tom when his anger flares up. His breathing becomes short and shallow when he's angry. Compare your breathing rate to Tom's breathing when he has one of his episodes. The short and shallow breathing is the same, but you feel anxious instead of angry. When you feel nervous or angry, slow and even breathing helps.

You decide to teach Tom slow and even breathing to see if it helps him calm down. You pick a time when he is mellow, such as after a bath.

You: "Tom, please sit on the bed. I want to teach you a special kind of breathing."

Tom: Tom climbs on the bed with a puzzled look.

You: "Great. Just like that. This is how big kids breathe when they get too upset. It makes them less angry."

Tom: Tom wants to be a big kid. You have his attention now.

You: "I'm going to lift my hands like this to breathe in."
Place your hands in front of your waist, palms down. Lift

them slowly, but not higher than your shoulders, as you breathe in.

"Then I'll lower my hands like this for breathing out."

Lower your hands in the same position back to your waist. Continue to breathe in and breathe out. Use the hand gestures each time.

Tom: Tom starts to copy your hand motions and breathes but has trouble slowing down to your speed.

You: "You don't need to do the hands, Tom. Just copy the breathing. You're doing great."

You speed up your breathing rate almost to match Tom's. As you keep practicing, gradually slow down your breathing. Slow breathing can be learned but takes many repetitions and practice sessions.

Tom: Tom yawns. "I feel sleepy."

You: "You did a terrific job."

Two things to remember: Slow breathing is relaxing, and the hand gestures signal Tom to slow his breathing down. Because slow breathing is relaxing, you might schedule your practice sessions at times when you want him to calm down and be more relaxed, such as at bedtime.

Later, you can use the hand gestures to prompt him to slow his breathing in social situations. It's like a secret code between the two of you. When you see him revving up, you can call his name, establish eye contact, and make the hand gestures. Tom will automatically slow down his breathing if you have practiced long enough.

This example shows how you can help your child self-regulate. But what if you don't catch the anger ramp-up in time?

Using Slow Breathing to Manage an Angry Episode

You're working when Tom explodes. He may have given you hints that he was about to erupt, but you didn't notice.

Recommendation

Consider this suggestion on how to repair the situation:

Tom: Tom is hitting his toy against the coffee table and yelling.

You: "Tom, please slow your breathing down. Come over to the couch and hit the toy on the couch."

Tom: Tom continues yelling and hitting.

You: "Tom, please come over to the couch."

Tom: Tom moves to the couch and hits his toy on the seat.

You: "Very good. Now watch me."

Tom: Tom hits and looks.

You: "Try to follow my breathing. When I breathe in, you breathe in. When I breathe out, you breathe out. Hit the toy when you breathe out. Like this."

       Demonstrate the instructions. You are using modeling and distracting methods. Hitting the toy on the couch and breathing out will require him to focus on the action in rhythm with his breathing.

Tom: Tom slows his breathing and hits the toy against the couch.

You: "Very good. Now let's try a little slower."

Tom: Tom slows his breathing down.

You: "That is so good."

Keep doing the slow, even breathing until you see him calm down. Slow breathing works well to calm the body. Exercise is another tool.

Exercise

Exercise is the best prevention for angry outbursts in children. A good workout reduces excess energy, which is why parents encourage their kids to play sports.

Another way to use exercise is when your child is already worked up and needs to dissipate some of the excess energy.

Using Exercise to Lower the Load of Anger

It's been too cold and stormy to go outside, and five-year-old Tom has cabin fever. He hasn't had a chance to get much exercise. His energy level is through the roof. You're working when he explodes.

Recommendation

You can use the following method to calm Tom's agitation:

Tom: Tom is yelling and throwing things.

You: "Let's get some exercise."

Tom: "*I want to go outside!*"

You: "We can't do that; it's too slippery and windy. You can race up and down the stairs. I can time you. We'll see how many laps you can do this time. You're getting pretty fast." You've done this before. This is your go-to method when you see Tom wound up and it's too late to go outside or the weather is harsh. You pull out your phone and open the timer app.

Tom: Tom runs to the bottom of the stairs and waits for you to say, "Go!"

You can devise your in-home activities to help your child discharge excess energy.

The thought-stopping and thought-replacement method is another option that works well with older children and adults.

Thought Stopping and Thought Replacement

Thoughts drive actions and emotions. If specific thoughts or beliefs make you angry, you can use the following method to reduce your emotional temperature. Thought stopping and thought replacement are great techniques for controlling your thinking. When you have a negative thought, replace it with something positive. For example, you can have a negative thought, such as, *I hate myself*. You then replace the thought with its opposite, *I like myself*.

Negative thinking can involve upsetting scenarios of past events or those that could happen.

The following are suggestions for explaining thought stopping and thought replacement to your older child or preteen:

- If you think about things that make you angry, change what you're thinking about. That will help you feel calmer and more cheerful.

- Your body reacts to a thought as if the event is happening in real time. If you think about how you got angry at Johnny yesterday, you will get angry all over again. Johnny didn't do anything wrong today. But you're full of anger as if he did.

- You feel all the body changes of anger, stress, and anxiety.

- If you keep thinking about the things that upset you and make you angry, you upset yourself repeatedly. Why would you want to do that to yourself? You're creating a pattern of negative thinking.

- To break up the pattern, you replace the negative thinking with something positive. Imagine yourself in a wonderful new situation in the future. Think of past vacations you enjoyed and replay them in your head. Think of making new friends. Imagine being great at something that you really enjoy. Use anything that puts a smile on your face and brightens your mood. When you find yourself in an upsetting thinking pattern, it's best to have a list of go-to positive storylines ready.

Help your children find positive thoughts or storylines that work for them. Here are some examples:

- Imagine meeting a new friend and hitting it off.
- Imagine getting a new friend who appreciates you.

- Think of a time when you were completely happy and carefree. Try to remember every detail.
- Imagine being good at a skill you would like to acquire.

Next is an example of how to use the method in an actual situation.

Example of a Preteen Who Worries About What Friends Think of Her

You notice that eleven-year-old Kay has been brooding a lot lately. She looks angry and upset much of the time. You've had a conversation with her and established that she worries excessively about what her friends say or don't say about her. Kay used to have a best friend, but they drifted apart, and she thinks about the breakup repeatedly. She focuses on how Tina caused the rift and recalls all the texts and conversations from the past. You decide that the fretting about the past is harming her.

Recommendation

Kay is in a pattern of negative thinking. Here is how you can teach her thought stopping and thought replacement.

You: "It upsets me to see you so angry and stressed all the time. I think you got into a pattern of worrying about the past and now can't escape it."

Kay: "I try not to think about it, but it's always there."

You: "How about if you think about things that make you smile? What are those things?"

Kay: "Going shopping for new clothes?" She says this hopefully.

You: "That won't work to stop the thoughts at night when you're trying to fall asleep."

Kay: "Oh. What then?"

You: "Do you remember a time when you were completely

relaxed, happy, or excited? Maybe a vacation? Maybe a concert? A softball game?"

Kay: "Yes. Remember the game when I hit a home run?"

You: "I do. What else? We need three scenarios you can replay in your head instead of the negative thoughts. Maybe a daydream?"

Kay: "Yes. I used to think about being an influencer like Carrie."

You: "That's good. We need one more thing. What about a vacation we took?"

Kay: "I liked Hawaii."

You: "Can you remember details, like the beach, ocean, and hotel?"

Kay: "Yes. The ocean was my favorite part."

You: "Perfect. Now I'll teach you the thought-stopping and thought-replacement method. When you find yourself thinking about a negative event, make yourself stop. Start thinking about the Hawaii vacation instead—all the details, including how the water felt, how the sand felt, and the sun and wind on your skin. Imagine looking at the ocean, the little boats, and the people on the beach. Boom! You find yourself back on the negative thought. Catch yourself. Stop and return to the Hawaii vacation. Each time your thoughts return to the negative, you pull yourself away and replace those negative thoughts with the memory of the game or your dream of being an influencer. It's like playing a tug-of-war with your thoughts. But you'll win."

Kay: "I can try."

The tips in this chapter are for things you can do at home. If your child's anger issues persist, please seek professional help. These methods may not work as well with neurodivergent (autistic) children. In these cases, the children may be so overstimulated that they cannot attend to any of your interventions. It's best to remove objects that can be broken or used to harm and any environmental triggers for the meltdown, then wait for it to subside.

Another emotion that overwhelms some children is depression. Depression in young children is often hidden under a layer of other behaviors.

THIRTY

Depression

Your curious, joyful, and talkative Marcie has become a snippy, tearful, and quiet child. She worries about her clothes and grades and avoids her friends. You've tried talking to her, but the problems she describes don't seem like a big deal, and you assured her that everything would be all right soon.

But it's been three months, and you're worried about the drastic change.

Depression is rare before the age of twelve. The literature shows a 1 to 2 percent incidence.

Young children do not present the classic signs of depression that you may be familiar with, so it's difficult to know when your child needs professional help. Here is a list of possible signs of behavior changes that can signal depression in young children:

- Crying
- Irritability
- Looking tired
- Drop in grades
- Angry outbursts
- Lack of motivation
- Behavior problems

- Headaches, stomachaches
- Worrying about school grades
- Worrying about what others think of them
- Low self-esteem and fretting over missteps
- Change in eating habits—eating less or more than before
- Defeated look—slumped shoulders, avoiding eye contact
- Changes in sleep schedule—sleeping a lot or an inability to sleep
- Lack of enjoyment in what used to please them or make them laugh

You may wonder why young children become depressed. After all, they don't have to worry about providing for the family or getting a good job.

Causes of Depression in Young Children

Excessive worrying is a hallmark of depression. Anything that makes children feel unwell, unloved, or unsafe causes them to worry and feel hopeless.

Here is a list of serious problems that affect children:

- Becoming victims of sexual abuse or violence or witnessing violence
- Rejection by parents or parents unavailable because of work or absence
- Chronic medical conditions, such as diabetes, lupus, or asthma
- Natural disasters or other causes of loss of home
- High-functioning autism
- Peer problems, bullying
- Gender identity issues
- Loss of a loved one
- Food insecurity
- Discrimination
- Early puberty

What Can Parents Do?

Spend more time with your child. Perhaps they have been sharing their problems, and you have assured them they will go away and not to worry.

It's time to take their problems seriously. Ask how they've tried to fix things and what happened. Be sympathetic. Avoid criticizing your child when they're hurting. This is not the time to say, "It's your own fault."

Ask if they want you to intervene. If so, what do they want you to do?

If they say they don't know what is wrong, ask if they feel unwell, like their battery is low.

Take them for a checkup with their doctor. Perhaps there is a hidden medical issue. The pediatrician can use questionnaires to do a basic depression assessment.

If there is no medical issue, start a conversation to help your child discuss possible concerns. Next is a list of questions you can ask.

Questions to Ask Your Child

Ensure you are in a quiet, private space when you have the conversation. Try to face your child when asking these important questions. Give them time to answer. Watch for facial expressions; their words may not match their mood. They may not have the words to describe their worries or inner experiences.

- Do you feel lonely?

- Has someone hurt you in any way?

- Do you feel like the schoolwork is too much?

- Is someone bullying you? Spreading rumors about you?

- Do you have trouble understanding the other kids at school?

- Are you worried or upset about something I've said or done?

- Did you hear or see something that is worrying you or scaring you?

- Do you feel as if the teachers or the kids don't like you, and you don't know why?

- Are you worried or upset about something that someone (Daddy, Grandma, Grandpa, your uncle, a teacher) has said or done?

- Do you feel as if someone is discriminating against you? Treating you like you don't belong in the group, school, or country?

End each conversation by asking what you can do to make things better. Does your child want you to intervene or prefer to handle the situation by themselves? Clearly, some of these situations need adult intervention.

When to Seek Therapy for Your Child

You may find that the issues your child is grappling with are more than you can handle or help them with. This is a time to seek professional mental health treatment.

Many times, the depression is hidden, and all you see is anxiety. Anxiety and depression co-occur in many cases.

THIRTY-ONE

Generalized Anxiety

Do you suspect your child suffers from anxiety? Are you wondering what you can do?

To help, you need to understand anxiety and why conquering fear is so hard. I'll begin with a description and finish with tips about things you can do to help your children.

Types of Anxiety Reactions

There is the anxiety of firsts. Children can react with fear to the first day of school or the first time giving a presentation in front of the class. The anxiety goes away once the situation becomes familiar.

This chapter focuses on anxiety states that don't go away. They stick around and repeat themselves. These anxieties can be crippling and may need professional intervention. The repeated anxiety states can be situational anxiety or phobias. Both may seem irrational, but the fear is real.

Here is a list of typical types of anxiety in children:

- School anxiety—refusal to go to school
- Separation anxiety—refusal to be away from you
- Social anxiety—refusal to mingle with children or adults

- Fear of flying
- Fear of heights
- Fear of public toilets
- Fear of closed places like elevators
- Fear of specific animals or insects, such as dogs, snakes, or spiders

What Do Anxiety and Panic Attacks Feel Like on the Inside?

Children can feel sped up, restless, tense, confused, shaky, jittery, weak, hot, flushed, nauseous, dizzy, or several sensations at once. The tension might cause jaw, neck, stomach, or chest pain. Generalized anxiety begins with a specific incident and spreads out to multiple situations and locations.

A panic attack is a feeling of overwhelming anxiety. The child cannot concentrate. All the symptoms listed previously are magnified. The child cannot control their thoughts and emotions. Panic attacks often seem to come out of nowhere and are generally not attached to an event or to a specific phobia.

What Do Anxious Children Look Like?

Your anxious child may look restless and shaky, with obvious perspiration. They display fast and shallow breathing, rapid speech, and a flushed face or neck. They may cling to you and attempt to avoid certain places or situations. Your child may also complain of stomach pain or feel weak and unable to sleep or think.

You might see extreme tantrums when they are unable to avoid overwhelming situations. Your child may appear preoccupied and avoid some places. You cannot distract them, and behavior charts aren't much help.

An Anxious Child's Effect on the Family

An anxious child can be crippling to the entire family. A child who refuses to go to school or day care disrupts your well-established morning routine. You miss work because you're dealing with your child. You juggle schedules. Everyone else in the family suffers neglect because of your anxious child.

If the behavior persists, you may find yourself avoiding certain things, such as public toilets, elevators, or your next-door neighbors who are walking their dogs. Daily life becomes strategic as you plan all activities around your anxious child to avoid tantrums.

Anxiety Spreads

Anxiety spreads like the wavelets created by throwing a rock into a calm body of water. If a child is nervous about something, the feeling can attach itself to a variety of new settings that did not trigger anxiety in the past.

Anxiety Triggered by a Dog Bite

A dog bites your child, and she develops a fear of dogs. You keep your child safe from dogs. One Saturday, the family goes to the neighborhood park, where many dog lovers walk their dogs. Your child becomes highly anxious and demands to go home. You try to calm her down, but she becomes hysterical, and you can feel a tantrum coming on. You take her home.

The following Saturday, the family plans a trip to the park. Your child refuses to go and pitches a fit. You stay home with her, and Dad takes the other kids to the park. The child's anxiety has now spread to include going to the park. Now the mere thought of going to the park triggers overwhelming anxiety.

Anxiety Is Illogical, but the Fear Is Real

Part of the brain's function is to protect us from harm. The brain is on the lookout for dangerous situations. When the brain perceives danger, certain chemicals are released to aid the person in fighting or fleeing. The brain is also careful to remember where dangerous situations are encountered to avoid them in the future.

And there you have it.

The dog bite is the original dangerous situation. The memory of the dog bite causes avoidance of potential dog situations. Anxiety at the park creates a memory of the park as a dangerous place. The tantrum is the fight response to avoid an overwhelming situation.

Thoughts are very powerful. Just imagining a potentially dangerous situation can be a trigger for extreme anxiety.

What Can You Do?

I recommend seeking professional help as soon as possible. If therapy is not an option, chapter 15 ("Emotional Regulation") and chapter 17 ("Relaxation Technique") can provide you with more tools to help your child.

The best way you can help at home is to practice slow breathing with your child. Emotions can alter breathing and make it short and shallow, but the process also works in reverse. If you slow your breathing, you can reduce the state of excitation in the body, thereby reducing anxiety.

If your child is anxious, take the time to sit with them and start the slow and even breathing process. It calms your excitement, and they can copy your mood. You become a model for how adults calm themselves when upset or overstimulated.

Pick a time when your child is calmer to teach slow and even breathing, as described in chapter 17. Practice the slow-breathing method often so that your child becomes good at it. When the anxiety comes, they'll have a ready tool. You are creating a new habit of self-calming. Explain to them that they can use slow breathing anywhere—at school, at the store, at the park, in the elevator, or on the playground. No one will know. It's their secret.

Chapter 17 provides step-by-step instructions on slow and even breathing. Chapter 15 provides examples of what to do if the emotions are already upon you.

Sometimes an anxiety state becomes entrenched as an extreme separation anxiety beyond the toddler stage.

THIRTY-TWO

Extreme Separation Anxiety

Help your toddler with extreme separation anxiety by gradually increasing their tolerance of separation through structured exercises. Your child can learn how to manage their anxiety without involving you in the process. Right now, you are their anxiety reducer. The exercises in this chapter can free you from this function.

Separation Anxiety

Separation anxiety is a normal developmental stage between six months and three years of age. You can't even go to the bathroom unescorted, or your child wails on the other side of the door, trying to establish contact. If your bathroom door has a space on the bottom, you can see an eye peeking under the door. They think you've gone away.

Very young children don't have object permanence. If you hide an object under a cup with them watching, they believe it's gone. They do not attempt to remove the cup to get to the object. If you go into another room and close the door, the child doesn't automatically know you are behind the door, even if they just watched you go through it.

Most babies develop object permanence by eight to fourteen months, but not for all situations. The anxious clinging usually subsides as your child develops object permanence because they understand you are behind the door and not gone forever.

However, separation anxiety can continue past age two. Here are some reasons:

- You, the parent, suffer from separation anxiety. You and your child reinfect each other with separation anxiety. Is this your situation? You may benefit from learning and applying relaxation techniques before you attempt to help your child.

- The anxiety response may have become a habit. Repeated behaviors and emotional reactions can easily become habits. The brain constantly streamlines and simplifies reactions, leading to habit formation.

- Personality style can also be a driving force. Some children attempt to control situations by overtly and passively manipulating their parents.

- Autistic and hyperactive children may suffer from separation anxiety if they lack object permanence past the age of three.

Regardless of the source of separation anxiety, the solution is the same.

Training Your Child to Tolerate Increasing Levels of Separation

Separation anxiety is driven by the inability to tolerate any anxiety. Your task is to help your child tolerate small amounts of anxiety for short periods.

Instead of saying, "I'm leaving for an hour, and you'll stay with Grandma," you set up separation exercises at your house in five-minute increments.

To ensure success, make a separation plan:

- Stay in the kitchen while your child goes to the living room, where they can see you, or let them pick another room where they can't see you but can hear you moving around.

- Give them a choice of doing the exercise with the door open or closed.

- What toys do they bring to their away place?

- How about a timer?

- Would they like a reward for doing the exercises? If so, what is the reward? Negotiate so that you don't bankrupt yourself.

Those choices give them a feeling of control. Start with ten five-minute training sessions per day. Set up the times and note everything on a daily schedule. Anxious children don't like surprises.

Explain why you are doing the exercises—to help them be less anxious. Avoid mentioning separation anxiety.

Explain the process slowly and clearly. Quiz your child as you speak to make sure they are following. Introducing a new regimen produces anxiety, and when the anxiety level is high, people don't listen well. You want to make sure they understand.

Begin the exercise the same day to avoid a twenty-four-hour panic about something new.

Exercise 1

Make sure your child understands that this is not a time-out. The training is to help them with away time. If they protest, ask if they want to be calmer and more cheerful.

1. They can take whatever toys or electronic devices they want to play with. The time starts when they get to their place.

2. Don't take them to their away place. They go there themselves, taking their comfort toys and a timer. Having choices gives them control.

3. In case of extreme anxiety, ask your child if they want to start with three- or five-minute sessions. Controlling their away time makes them feel more secure in the situation.

4. Show the schedule to your child and tell them it's time for them to pick a spot for their away time.

5. If they can't manage to stay there the whole time, it's OK. Smile and say, "That's a good start. Next time, you'll do better. You're in training. We'll keep practicing."

6. For the next session on the same day, tell your child they can pick the same spot for their away time or a different one. The timer starts when they're settled in the place.

7. Note their success on the schedule.

8. Reward your child with praise.

Expect to do many, many, many repetitions of the first exercise to lower the anxiety level.

Before you move to the next exercise, make sure they can tolerate five minutes in another room with the door closed. You want to ensure that separation is overlearned through repetition.

When five minutes is comfortable, move on to exercise 2.

Exercise 2

Introduce the second exercise by telling them the following:

1. "You're so good at five minutes that we can extend the time. Would you like to make it ten minutes or fifteen minutes? It's ten times a day for ten-minute sessions or eight times a day for fifteen-minute sessions."

2. When your child is comfortable with fifteen minutes eight times a day, challenge them to thirty-minute away sessions.

3. Tell them that if they can manage thirty minutes in their away place, they only have to do it four times a day.

4. Keep a written schedule.

5. Mark successes.

6. Reward your child with praise.

For exercise 2, you top out at thirty-minute sessions. When your child tolerates thirty minutes, you can move on to the next exercise.

Exercise 3

After praising their progress, explain that the next exercise involves them staying at home while you leave for fifteen minutes.

1. The adult who stays with the child can be any adult with whom your child feels comfortable.

2. If your child becomes anxious and asks to return to five minutes of you being gone, then start with five-minute sessions. By now, your child has better control of their anxiety, so there's less fuss.

3. Practice several times a day.

4. Note successes on the schedule.

5. Give praise to your child.

When fifteen-minute absences are well tolerated, move to thirty minutes. Exercise 3 tops out at one hour.

Exercise 4

Now you're moving the training outside the home by taking your child to someone else's house and leaving for fifteen minutes while your child stays.

1. If your child is flooded with anxiety, give them the option to decide how long you'll be gone. Bring their comfort toys and a timer so that they can time your absence.

2. When a shorter time is well tolerated, you can do several fifteen-minute absences, fifteen minutes apart.

3. When fifteen minutes is well tolerated, move to thirty-minute absences, then to one hour, then longer. Stretch this phase over several days.

4. Create a schedule for this exercise.

5. Mark successes.

6. Give your child praise.

Exercise 4 tops out at four hours.

Exercise 5

Exercise 5 involves going to school.

1. Take your child to see the school when no kids are there.

2. Next, try to arrange a school visit when the children are there.

3. Point out things your child likes so that they know the school contains some familiar items and playground equipment.

4. If you see your child tensing up or note that their breathing is short and shallow, remind them to breathe slowly and evenly.

5. After the visit, play school at home.

6. You can be the teacher. Tell your child they can ask anything about the class, the kids, or what to do. Their questions can tell you what worries them.

7. Explain everything.

8. Have them practice raising their hand to ask questions or use the restroom.

9. Assure your child that everyone starts not knowing anything. All the kids have to learn where things are and what they're supposed to do.

10. The teacher explains everything.

11. When dropping your child off at school, make sure you are relaxed.

12. Play relaxing music on the way to school.

13. At school, hand your child off to the teacher or someone who can show them where to go.

14. Tell your child, "I'll pick you up at three p.m. I'll be waiting by the car. The teacher will tell you where to go."

Why the Approach Works

The exercises combine predictability, consistency, choice, repetition, overlearning, and reinforcement to help your child increase their tolerance for anxiety. As a side benefit, your child's ability to manage their anxiety also improves.

You can stop being their go-to anxiety reducer.

A rare anxiety-driven problem for young children is obsessive-compulsive disorder.

THIRTY-THREE

Obsessive-Compulsive Disorder

If your child suffers from extreme anxiety, they may also suffer from obsessive-compulsive disorder (OCD). This disorder is relatively rare in children. Massive anxiety fuels all types of OCD behaviors.

OCD has made its way into everyday jargon. People say to one another, "Oh, you're so OCD!" when they mean you are too organized, structured, rigid, or inflexible.

That is not OCD.

The Symptoms of OCD

The symptoms are recurring, disturbing, intrusive (obsessive) thoughts that cannot be controlled and compel a child to engage in specific and repetitive corrective actions. If the child is stopped from performing the actions or tries to stop themselves, they are flooded with overwhelming anxiety.

The thoughts and the actions the child is compelled to perform to ward off the anxiety take up a lot of time and are disruptive to daily life. The whole process makes it hard to concentrate at school.

Adults suffering from OCD realize their actions are illogical, but they cannot stop themselves.

Intrusive thoughts alone are not a sign of OCD.

People may have intrusive thoughts about something they consider pleasurable but decide to give up, such as comfort foods, sugary snacks, or foods they are allergic to. These thoughts are not foreign, sinful, repulsive, or scary to them. They are thoughts of things they enjoy but decided to give up.

OCD is very different, especially in children. Next are some examples of true intrusive thoughts and the accompanying compulsions.

Obsessions and Compulsions in Children

Intrusive thoughts (obsessions) cause certain behaviors (compulsions). *Fear of losing or forgetting to do something* leads to checking and rechecking or doing and redoing—for example, checking their homework or artwork repeatedly, erasing, correcting, and erasing again.

Fear of germs or illness leads to repeated handwashing or refusing to eat at restaurants.

The extreme *need to have things in symmetrical order* leads to moving objects on desks. For example, they cannot start homework or work on projects until the items on the desk are lined up in a specific way. Another example is a sequence of events that must be performed in an exact order or they cannot be done at all.

Fear of acting on aggressive thoughts toward others can lead to repeated ritual behaviors. Sometimes the ritual involves silent counting. Other times the child may walk over cracks in the pavement or take two steps forward and three steps back. At times the rituals are more involved, such as walking along the walls of hallways and turning to the right or left at intervals.

Fear of acting on intrusive, unwanted, sinful thoughts, such as violent thoughts, can lead to ongoing praying, repeating certain words silently, or superstitious behaviors to ward off the frightening thoughts.

Children do not see the illogic of their intrusive thoughts or actions.

Intrusive thoughts are not the only symptoms of OCD. There are also involuntary actions.

Symptoms That Look and Sound Like Tic Disorder

Not all children with OCD experience tics, but some might. The tics can be unusual and can manifest as repetitive eye movements, head and shoulder jerking, making faces, grunting, or throat clearing. As in tic disorders, these movements cannot be controlled.

Getting Stuck or Freezing in Place

Getting stuck or freezing in place means a child cannot perform a normal function because if they try to do the next step, they get flooded with anxiety. The freezing in place can happen while crossing the street, walking through doorways, getting in or out of the car, or picking up a pen to write or draw. The child gets stuck and stands or sits there, motionless.

I've seen this with autistic children who also suffer from OCD.

Family Members of OCD Sufferers

Children try to make you part of their ritualistic behavior. They may tell you to do things in a specific order or insist you tuck them in at night in a certain way. You can see your child is anxious, and you want to help.

However, I recommend against complying with such requests. Although participating in the ritual may ease their anxiety for a minute, other demands to involve you in their rituals will follow. You will not get anything done, and your child will remain anxious.

Treatment for OCD

Massive anxiety fuels the whole system. The intrusive thoughts (obsessions) trigger the anxiety, and the behaviors (compulsions) are meant to ease the fear.

Perhaps you think all you have to do is get rid of your child's anxiety and you'll get rid of OCD. Unfortunately, it's not that easy because the intrusive thoughts remain.

Many self-help methods are floating around on the internet, but they focus on the illogic of intrusive thoughts and teach you how to ignore the thoughts while reducing anxiety. Such exercises won't help children who don't see their intrusive thoughts as illogical.

There are psychiatric medications that help alleviate or reduce the symptoms. I recommend you consult a psychiatrist, as well as a therapist who specializes in OCD.

Another condition that often triggers anxiety is slow processing speed.

THIRTY-FOUR

Slow Processing Speed

Does your child face learning challenges, struggle to start and complete tasks, or have a hard time keeping up in social situations?

These issues can be due to slow thought-processing speed.

When you spend time with a group of children, you'll notice that some react to questions faster than others. Some jump into play quickly, whereas others stay on the sidelines and evaluate the situation. We tend to think of the ones who respond quicker as bright and those who hang back and don't engage in play right away as shy.

But are those signs of intelligence and shyness? The quick response to a question can be due to the child's fast processing speed of what is heard and the corresponding speedy formulation of an answer. The apparent shyness can be due to a child's slow processing of what is seen and heard, followed by a slow processing of the appropriate response.

Next, I discuss some indicators of slow processing speed. Your child may have a slow processing speed if they do the following:

- You call them and they don't react.
- They appear to have no awareness of time.
- They appear lazy because it takes them forever to get anything done.

- They appear intelligent in some areas but fail in timed tasks.
- They knew the material the night before but did poorly on the test.
- You give them three-step instructions, and they remember to do only one of the things.
- They have many interests and good ideas but need help with their homework assignments.

These behaviors can be part of several diagnostic categories, such as learning disabilities, attention deficit hyperactivity disorder (ADHD) of the inattentive subtype, and autism, but slow thought-processing speed can also exist as a stand-alone issue.

Recommendation

To help your child, try the following:

You call them and they don't react. They may respond if you don't jump in with another question right away. Wait a minimum of thirty seconds before you say anything else. Watch for body language that shows they heard you.

Call them again. Make sure you say their name and speak louder. Wait a minimum of thirty seconds before saying anything else. If there is no reaction, touch them lightly and repeat their name.

They appear to have no sense of time. You can help by keeping a standing weekday schedule. Make it a visual schedule to be posted in their room. The schedule must include the time to start each activity and the allotted time to complete it.

To decide how much time to give each activity, stand there with a timer and time your child as they do each activity. On the weekday schedule, list wake-up time, getting dressed time, breakfast time, homework time, shower time, and relaxing time. Make sure you stick to the schedule and hold the child to it as well.

They appear lazy because it takes them forever to get anything done. What looks like procrastination can be a time management problem. Because of their lack of sense of time, they tend to misjudge how long it takes them to complete a task. Start with the weekday schedule you created, which has the number of minutes you expect them to take to complete the task.

Next, train them to start and complete a task within the time frame. You are teaching them to be time watchers. If they have ten minutes to get dressed and brush their teeth, you help by standing there with a timer and calling out, "You have nine more minutes. You have eight more minutes..."

Plan to repeat the process until they succeed in fewer than ten minutes. Then let them control the timer so that they learn to time themselves. Your job is done when they can manage clock watching on their own for all their tasks. Timed task skills must be overlearned to become a habit.

They appear intelligent in some areas but fail in timed tasks. Some kids can complete tasks and do well if given enough time. However, our world is moving at a faster pace these days.

School tests can be a problem area for your child. If your child does well on homework but struggles to complete schoolwork or tests, you can request a school psychological evaluation to test for processing speed. If their test results indicate slow processing speed, the psychologist will recommend extended test time to accommodate your child.

They knew the material the night before but did poorly on the test. Some children with slow processing speeds and time management issues get anxious during testing, and the information flies out of their heads.

If half the test was done correctly but your child didn't finish, you can assume it's a processing-speed issue. If anxiety is added to the mix, mistakes might occur throughout the test.

If you give them three-step instructions, they remember to do only one of them. If you speak fast and your child is slow at absorbing what they hear, they hear only the first thing. You kept talking while they were processing the first instruction. Slow your speech, keep the instructions simple, and ask them to repeat your words.

If they struggle to repeat the instructions, try again. This time, give your child these instructions:

1. Empty the trash from all the trash cans in the house into this bag.
2. Put the bag in the big trash can.
3. Take the big trash can to the street.

Have them repeat the instructions. Don't send them off until they've memorized the instructions.

They have many interests and good ideas but need help with their homework assignments. The assignments may be overwhelming for a child with slow processing speed. Teach your child to focus on one task at a time. Have them work at ten- to fifteen-minute intervals, depending on their age and focusing ability.

For example, for a page of math problems, have them cover all but the problems they're working on right then. If they're doing research, make sure they're not distracted by things that are interesting to them but that are not part of the research project.

The Emotional Toll on the Whole Family

A child with slow processing speeds affects the whole family. Those family members with fast processing speeds feel frustrated. Siblings may become irritated or tease your other child, resulting in yelling, emotional outbursts, and delays. Strife slows down your slow-processing child even more.

The whole family must slow down when speaking to your slow processor. Say one thing at a time. Relax. Yelling isn't going to speed them up.

Getting Professional Help

If you suspect your child has a slow processing speed, consider doing the following:

- Request testing by the school psychologist. A psychological report can trigger the school to provide accommodations to help your child succeed.

- You can get neuropsychological testing done privately through insurance or pay for it yourself. Whoever does the testing explains all the tests and results and recommends what you can do at home to help your child. The report includes educational recommendations you can share with the school.

- Your child may have additional diagnoses, such as ADHD, autism, anxiety, or depression. In that case, you are referred to the appropriate mental health professionals who can assist you and your child with additional treatments.

- Find an audiologist who can test for auditory-processing disorder and recommend ways to help your child based on that diagnosis.

- For more in-depth discussion on the topic, read *Bright Kids Who Can't Keep Up* by Ellen Braaten and Brian Willoughby (2014).

You Can Do It!

To get results, the whole family needs to learn to slow down when speaking to the slow processors in the family—there might be more than one. Break up instructions into chunks. Say one thing at a time. Breathe. Relax. Avoid yelling because extreme stress slows things down even more.

Slow processing speed leads to stress, and stress may drive your older child to experiment with stress-reducing pills or other substances offered by kids at school.

THIRTY-FIVE

Your Preteen and Substance Abuse

Why did I include a chapter about substance abuse in a book geared toward the parents of two- to eleven-year-olds?

There are three reasons:

1. The issues that make kids susceptible to substance abuse arise early in life. If they are not resolved or improved, and if the kids feel unsupported, they may turn to substance abuse to cope with the pressure of daily life.

2. Preteens are curious about the world and new experiences. They also bond with friends, and peer pressure becomes a new force in their lives. They begin to listen more to peers and less to adults.

3. Some kids become involved with alcohol, marijuana, and pills before the age of eleven. When I interviewed patients, I asked about their childhood experiences and their earliest involvement with drugs and alcohol. The earliest intentional use of alcohol was at age seven. Some may experiment, but

others continue and are at risk of becoming addicted before they get to high school.

Are Some Kids More at Risk of Developing Substance Abuse Issues?

The answer to this question is yes.

Some kids are especially vulnerable to getting entangled in substance abuse. The following list contains contributing issues you can work on:

- Peer rejection
- Academic problems
- Mental health problems
- Puberty, developmental changes
- Moving, family separation, divorce
- Other family members using substances
- Going from elementary to middle school to high school

Poverty and living in a neighborhood where "everyone does it" are blamed for kids' substance abuse. I didn't include those in the list because you may not be able to do anything to fix your living situation.

Parental support, strong family bonds, and mentors in your child's lives are the glue that keeps them intact and less susceptible to unwanted outside influences.

Help your child to fortify themselves against stress.

Peer Rejection Hurts

Kids need at least one good friend. If your child is socially awkward, it's up to you to arrange playdates, look for kids with similar interests, and befriend other parents whose kids may be a good match. Make every effort to ensure your child has a buddy. Supervise, assist, and teach your child how to play games they may enjoy.

Do you have a child who prefers to be alone? If they have language, ask them if they feel lonely. You may be surprised by the answer.

A group using drugs accepts anyone who uses or smokes with them. Some kids fall into that belonging trap. But the problem begins much earlier in life.

Academic Problems

If your child struggles to learn, ensure they get all the support they need from the school. You can be the cheerleader and the helper. It's hard to be in a class if you are a child who feels confused and unable to learn like the other kids. After a few years of those types of experiences, your child can feel dumb, angry, anxious, depressed, and unmotivated. That's when they seek relief from those feelings.

Help your child find activities they are good at to improve their self-image. Try drawing, painting, crafts, singing, woodworking, drama, or a sport. What does your child like watching on YouTube? Is that something they could do well with effort and practice?

Mental Health Problems

If your child develops depression or anxiety or shows early aggressive behavior, seek professional help. Your child may be reacting to events in their life you know nothing about. If you don't help them deal with their emotional scars, they may turn to substance abuse for relief from bad feelings.

Puberty and Developmental Changes

If your child doesn't like change or has sensitivity issues, they may struggle with the body changes of puberty. They may hate their new body. The constant sense of not feeling right and always being uncomfortable creates negative thoughts about who they've become.

Nowadays, kids are going through puberty earlier. Talk to your child about body changes and what to expect. Don't depend on the school's health class.

Substance-Using Family Members

An older sibling or cousin who is drinking alcohol or using drugs may share them with your younger child. Drug and alcohol availability is a factor when kids begin experimenting early. If you have prescription medications for anxiety or pain, make sure they are out of reach of your kids.

Moving, Family Separation, and Divorce

Any changes in the living environment can lead to feelings of insecurity. Your child has no part in decision-making; they simply get uprooted from a familiar environment.

Please discuss any moves and separations with your child, focusing on how they will be affected and how you plan to make the move easier. Let them pack their own belongings—even if you have to repack everything. Let them keep some items from their current living situation.

Divorce is the hardest. For details, please read chapter 27 for more on children of divorce.

Going from Elementary School to Middle School and High School

Starting a new school is stressful for any child and scary for others. You can help by arranging an early tour of the new school. Take your child to the new school, get a map of the school, look for the classrooms on their class schedule, walk around the school, look for the cafeteria, and find where the bus pickup is. Or if you're doing the pickup, show your child where you'll be waiting.

When Parents Drink Alcohol and Use Drugs

If you use drugs or drink regularly, you'll have a hard time convincing your child not to do the same. Your child will grow up thinking everyone does it.

Your child is in the process of becoming an adult. They begin by copying you.

I once had a father tell me he stopped smoking marijuana and doing other drugs when his son got into drugs and he saw firsthand what drugs did to his son. His son became a reflection of himself.

What You Can Do to Keep Your Kids Off Drugs

The campaigns "Just Say No" and "This Is Your Brain on Drugs" sounded reasonable and catchy, but they didn't work.

Schools are tasked with policing drug and pill distribution in school, but they can't catch everyone. I once asked a high school patient of mine what makes kids popular, and he replied, "Selling drugs." This is not what a parent wants to hear.

You can't depend on other parents to keep your kids from smoking marijuana, using drugs, or drinking. Some parents think if they provide alcohol and marijuana at home, the kids are less likely to look elsewhere. The same parents may extend such hospitality to other people's kids.

It's up to you to arm your kids with the conviction that they just don't do certain things, such as lie, steal, drink alcohol, or use drugs.

Open conversations, caring family relationships, protection from unwanted influences, limit setting, and enforcement of consequences are the primary defenses against your child getting involved in pill taking, alcohol consumption, and drug use.

How to Have Open Conversations

You may wonder, If "Just Say No" and scare tactics about the consequences of substance abuse don't work, what do I talk about?

Encourage your child to talk to you about everything that happens during the day—not only at school. Be sympathetic. Always be on their side, even when they're wrong. You want to be a safe person to confide in when they encounter a confusing situation.

Later, when they are calmer, you can refer to the confusing situation and say, "We can't change other people. What could you have done differently so that the situation didn't blow up?"

When they come home in a mood, you can start by saying, "You're not your usual cheerful self." If they don't answer right away, be quiet. Give them time to process what happened so that they can tell you about the incident. At a later time, you can say, "You seemed to be in a bad mood before. Did something happen? Can I help?"

If pills or drugs are offered at school, your child has to be able to say, "No, thank you," and be comfortable with that, no matter what their peers say.

How Substance Abuse Seeps into Your Child's Life

It is rare for anyone to become an addict overnight. It begins with experimentation.

Consider these common scenarios: A friend may offer them a pill to help them do well on a test, sleep better, or alleviate anxiety. Children see the older kids vaping and taking pills and hear them talking about drinking. These activities and conversations are secretive, and there is a sense of danger of getting caught. They want to be an older kid, so they listen to the stories.

Here are some signs of a possible substance abuse problem in children:

- Unusual health issues
- Abrupt changes in friends
- Sudden changes in behavior
- Becoming secretive and lying
- No longer caring about appearance
- Loss of interest in favorite activities

- Change in eating and sleeping habits
- Worsening relationships with family members
- Problems with school conduct and performance

If you see any of these signs, you can assume something is off. This is a time to initiate a conversation.

How to Have a Conversation with Your Child About Substance Abuse

Your Mia has been showing some of the behaviors and health issues listed in the previous section. When she was at school, you searched her room and found vapes in the trash. You decide to take her to the doctor and ask to have her blood tested for drugs and medications.

Recommendation

The following conversations can serve as a road map on how to approach this difficult topic:

You: "You're different lately. You avoid us, you dropped your best friend, you're always in your room, you hardly eat anything, and you don't look well."

Mia: "I'm fine. Leave me alone."

You: "You're not fine. I worry. I see big changes. I'm concerned that something is wrong. Maybe you're sick. I'll make an appointment with the doctor."

Mia: "Oh, OK. I do feel weak."

The doctor's visit reveals Mia is anemic, and there is a trace of Xanax in her blood but nothing else. The doctor talks to Mia about eating a more balanced diet and asks you to get her some iron pills. She mentions Mia's blood showed she's been exposed to Xanax and gently encourages her to avoid taking pills furnished by friends. On the way home:

You: "Let's stop at the store and get the iron pills."

Mia: "OK."

You: "I hope the pills help you feel better, but the doctor recommended a more varied diet. What is your plan for eating healthier meals? I had anemia once when I went on a crazy diet."

Mia: "What kind of diet?"

You: "I think it was the grapefruit diet. I was on many diets when I was growing up. I loved cakes and chips best, but that made me gain weight, so I was always trying to lose weight."

Mia: "Did you smoke?"

You: "No. My parents smoked. That didn't look cool."

Mia: "Did you vape?"

You: "No. They didn't have vapes back then. They had marijuana, but I was really against smoking anything. My parents were always smoking."

Mia: "Did your friends smoke?"

You: "Yes. My friend Tania started smoking her parents' cigarettes. She tried to talk me into smoking, but I said no. I asked her not to smoke around me."

Mia: "Was she still your friend?"

You: "Yes, until she started smoking marijuana. Then it was hard to talk to her because she just wanted to sit around and smoke. She didn't want to do anything. So I found other friends."

Mia: "Did you take diet pills?"

You: "A friend gave me a diet pill. It made me zip around and not be interested in eating. Then the pill wore off, and I felt tired. I asked my friend what it was, and she said it was speed. I knew speed was addictive, so I never took it again."

Mia: "Did your friend keep taking it?"

You: "Yes. She got super skinny and started acting moody. She stopped being fun. After that, I stayed away from people who smoked and used drugs. Do your friends offer each other pills or vapes?"

Mia: "Yes, some."

You: "Have you tried anything?"

Mia: "Yes. I tried vaping."

You: "Tell me about the first time you tried it. Did you feel pressured to vape?"

Mia: "No. Some girls were smoking in the bathroom, and Jade offered me a puff. I wasn't pressured, just curious."

You: "What did you think?"

Mia: "It was OK. I didn't like the flavor."

You: "Did you try other flavors? Do you have a favorite?"

Mia: "Yes. I like the watermelon."

You: "Do you think you'll be vaping at my age?"

Mia: "No!"

You: "Does vaping make you feel older and more sophisticated?"

Mia: "A lot of older girls do it."

You: "Did you try any pills?"

Mia: "Yes. I was nervous about the poster presentation, and a girl gave me a pill."

You: "Did you know what it was?"

Mia: "No."

You: "Did it help with the presentation?"

Mia: "Not really. I didn't practice at home, so I didn't do well. But I wasn't nervous."

You: "We're at the store. Think about what healthy foods you want to eat so that we can buy those."

This example was of an information-gathering conversation. You began with self-disclosure so that Mia was comfortable sharing information. Notice that you were never judgmental of Mia, her friends, or her actions. You focused on sharing your experiences and feelings and asking if she experienced the same.

A Story About a Friend Taking Pills

Your child may come to you with a story about another kid taking pills or vaping. They've never brought the subject up before.

Look out! Danger ahead. Listen carefully.

At the end of the story, be nonjudgmental about the other child. Focus on your feelings and worries. Try to steer the conversation to ways your child can respond if offered pills, marijuana, or vapes. Have them problem-solve by practicing different scenarios. You can help if they need more ideas. "You can tell the kid the price would be too high. Or that your parents always find out, and they are crazy and give super-long punishments. It's not worth the trouble."

Instead of saying, "You're too young," ask, "Why do you think kids do those things?" If your child runs out of ideas, you can offer, "Do they think it makes them more grown-up? Do you think it makes them seem older? Do they think it's cool? Do you think it's cool? Are they worried their friends will make fun of them if they don't go along with the group?"

Then you can describe your feelings and worries. "I worry you may be talked into using pills or marijuana, drinking alcohol, or vaping. Once you start, it's hard to stop, and then you can end up with a bad habit. I worry about that a lot."

Are you concerned about the possibility of your innocent babies getting snagged by drugs? You probably are. Hopefully, you have nothing to worry about, but it helps to have a plan just in case.

What to Do If Your Child Dabbles in Substance Abuse

Discuss your concern with the other main caregivers for your child. Include all the caregivers in the discussion, even if you are divorced or separated. Find out how each caregiver feels about such experimentation and if it warrants consequences. Suppose all the caregivers don't want the child to use drugs or alcohol throughout high school. Your child needs to know. If you decide it's OK at some point, your child needs to know this too.

My recommendation is to go with the strictest parent. A united front is essential.

At the end of the discussion, plan how to present your feelings and worries to your children. Write it out. A short paragraph is best.

Next, come up with a plan for consequences if your talk doesn't do the trick and your child does drink or use marijuana or pills. I recommend the following:

1. First time using or drinking: Have a calm discussion and remind them of the expectations and consequences.
2. Second incident: Remove one favorite activity for two months.
3. Third incident: Remove one favorite activity for four months.
4. Fourth incident: Remove two favorite activities for four months.
5. Fifth incident: Remove two favorite activities for eight months.

Notice that the consequences increase exponentially. I wrote *favorite activity* because favorites change over time. Common favorites are gaming, going to the mall, using social media, or using their phone.

Does it sound harsh? Your child needs to know you mean business if you don't want them experimenting. The threat of severe consequences can help them say, "No, thank you."

Present the Results of the Discussion to Your Child

Dabbling in marijuana and pills is such an important topic with many negative consequences. I recommend you discuss it in the presence of all caregivers. Preteens feel omnipotent and don't understand how addiction works, so they think experimenting is OK.

Recommendation
Present your worries and your expectations. Next, share the list of consequences. Ask if they want a written copy of the consequences.

Expect an insulted response.

Kid: "But I didn't do any of those things!"

You: "We're happy to hear that. We also know you're of the age when kids begin experimenting with all sorts of things. We prefer you don't experiment with alcohol, pills, marijuana, and whatever else is offered. We used to be kids, and we know what peer pressure and wanting to copy bigger kids is like. Hopefully, the consequence list can help you say no when the time comes."

Kid: Sigh. "OK. Can I go now?"

Your child will face many dangers as they grow up. Hopefully, substance experimentation or abuse won't tempt them. But there is another danger that lurks in some children's lives, a danger that is beyond their control—potential child molesters. This is where you have to step up to protect them.

THIRTY-SIX

Child Molesters

Molestation and victimization are not things that happen to "other kids."

Being aware and proactive helps you to arm your child.

Your child is at risk.

Hearing about molestation is stomach churning and can make you angry, sad, and sick all at once. I don't blame you if your first instinct is to stop reading. But I urge you to keep on. Think of your child falling prey to such people. At least read the first five sections of this chapter so that you can recognize the signs.

The practice of child molestation is not new. What is new is that we can now talk openly about it, and some children even feel safe enough to report the abuse. Later, I'll discuss why some children don't report abuse and when to raise your antenna and start asking questions.

These days, the media focus is shifting to online victimization of children, but in-person molestation still occurs.

You may have experienced a single or repeated molestation by a family member or other "trusted" adult or teen in the community yourself.

How to Tell if Your Child Has Been Molested

Have your antenna up when someone pays too much attention to your child. Here are some other signs:

- Sexual themes in play or artwork

- Sudden onset of headaches and tummy aches

- Knowledge of sexual behavior beyond their years

- Bedwetting or soiling after having been toilet trained

- Trying to avoid specific individuals, including family members

- Making statements or asking questions about secrets and games

- Trying to avoid certain situations and looking upset or angry if you try to force them

- Sudden changes in mood or behavior, such as becoming unusually quiet, distant, clingy, fearful, zoned out, distracted, aggressive, or destructive

Preteens react with these behaviors:

- Substance abuse
- Problems with friends
- Self-isolation and depression
- Changes in eating, sleeping, or hygiene
- Aggression, destructive behaviors, or truancy
- Self-harming behaviors, such as cutting or thoughts of suicide

Perhaps your child had already experienced molestation. They are not themselves, but you can't tell what has happened. You ask questions but get vague answers. Whether your child described molestation or you suspect molestation, reach out to medical professionals.

What to Do When You Suspect or Confirm Molestation

Take your child to a medical facility or emergency room to be checked for any damage to their body. Ask your child to repeat what they told you. Medical staff may be better at asking questions. Parents have a hard time with the details. It's hard to listen to what happened to your child.

Following the interview, the medical staff must write a report of the incident and refer the case to Child Protective Services and the police.

The reason I recommend getting the child checked medically is because there might be some physical damage, and they can collect semen samples in the case of rape.

Take your child to a medical facility even if they say only that someone "touched" them. Children use *touching* to describe all sorts of acts because they might not have the language to explain what actually happened to them.

Do Molesters Stop Doing It Once They Are Exposed?

Parents whose children have been molested by someone within the home think yelling at the molester will stop the behavior.

It doesn't.

Some parents and organizations believe that once the molester is caught, they'll stop molesting.

They won't.

Did you know that if you are aware of your child's molestation, don't report the abuse, and don't stop the molestation, you are considered an accomplice?

How can you protect your child?

Ways to Protect Your Child from Child Molesters

Nurture a positive relationship with your child to shield them from harm. Your child needs to know you are always on their side. No matter what happens, you're there for them. Explain that your job is to protect them when they feel threatened in any way.

Teach your young child the following rules:

- Do not talk to strangers.
- Do not follow strangers.
- Do not let strangers touch you or tickle you.
- Do not accept snacks or treats from strangers.
- Do not let anyone touch you on your private parts.
- Tell me if anyone tickles you when you tell them to stop.
- If someone tries any of those things, you have to tell me right away.

Define a stranger as someone Mommy and Daddy don't know.

To explain the concept of private parts, draw a picture of a child and circle the private parts. A stick figure is fine.

The stranger idea is a difficult concept for little ones. My friend's daughter was four years old when she was spotted talking to a stranger. The person turned out to be a neighbor they hadn't met yet. When my friend admonished her daughter for talking to a stranger, she protested, "He's not a stranger; I told him my name."

Teach your preteen the following guidelines:

- Do not let anyone touch your private parts when you don't want them to.

- Come to me with any concerns. I'm here for you, even if you made the wrong choices.

- Do not let anyone get into your space if you don't want them to. Everyone has a personal space or boundary, which is approximately your extended arm's length. If they violate your personal space, move away from them.

- If you're supposed to be in a group and a coach or teacher tries to separate you for one-on-one help or training after school hours, say, "No, thank you. I have to go home."

- Do not post anything online or send anything via phone messaging you don't want to see on the evening news. There are no secrets online.

- Anything you send out electronically stays in the web universe *forever*.

- When you send something via Snapchat, the message may be erased, but the other person can take a screenshot and save the message or photo.

- Avoid doing anything that requires you to be secretive. If you have to hide an activity, it's usually a poor choice at any age.

Reading all this, you may wonder how molesters get access to children.

How Do Molesters Get Access to Children?

Molesters can be found in churches among clergy or support staff, youth groups, youth camps, coaching staff, schools, extended-family homes, and in your own home.

Churches used to be havens for molesters because they insisted on handling the abuse internally, often overlooking the victim and transferring the offender to another parish. The reasoning behind this response is selfish: Such organizations want to maintain the impression that your children are safe in their care and do anything to keep up the facade, with victims ending up paying the price.

Why do child molesters like to associate themselves with church groups or squeaky-clean organizations, such as the Boy Scouts? Because parents believe churchgoers to be God-fearing people who would never think of harming a child.

One child molester told me he picks church youth groups because the parents are naive. The scandals that rocked the Catholic Church and the Boy Scout organization are proof that no place is truly safe.

What about your home? You love your child. You would never harm them, and you assume others are like you. Not everyone is like you. Your home may not be safe either. This is sad but true in many children's lives.

Children have been molested by parents, parents' partners, foster parents, guardians, older siblings, aunts, uncles, cousins, grandparents, friends of the family, babysitters, and neighbors.

Should you distrust everyone and keep your child locked up at home under your watchful eye? No. But you do need to teach your child what to look out for and what to do if someone tries to touch them on their private parts or take pictures of them without their clothes on.

Next is a discussion of what makes kids especially vulnerable to molestation.

Victim Profile

The common victim profile includes children who exhibit these behaviors:

- Don't like to rock the boat

- Try to keep the family together at all costs

- Have a disturbed relationship with their parents

- Have parents who are too busy to care for them

- Are too young to have the words to tell what happened to them

- Accept gifts and special treats after each episode of molestation

- Are told the molestation is their fault because they were being sexy

- Can't count on their addicted parents to do anything to stop the abuse

- Are told they'll go to jail if they ever tell anyone what happened to them

- Are afraid the family will look bad if the abuse becomes public knowledge

- Are told their parents will go to hell if they say anything about what happened to them

- Believe that if they allow the abuser to victimize them, they will leave their siblings alone

- Lie and misbehave and are often at odds with their parents, who could protect them if they believed what the children were telling them

What about children and preteens who have a good relationship with their parents? Why don't they tell?

Why Much of Child Abuse Still Goes Unreported

Child victims and adults who were victimized as children don't like to remember the molestation. They try to forget. But the molestation can never be erased from memory. A part of them always remembers, leading to unexpected emotional experiences and reactions they don't connect to the abuse experience. The primary lingering effects are anxiety, depression, and substance abuse. Some may even disassociate (zone out).

Victims grow up feeling vulnerable and unprotected. Because abuse leads to a lack of trust, they grow up with trust issues. Depending on the nature of the abuse, they can grow up fearful of sexual activity or become promiscuous. All these issues cause lifelong problems in relationships.

Here are some of the reasons why children don't report the abuse:

- Guilt
- Shame
- Bribes by the perpetrator

- Fear of retaliation by the abuser
- Fear that no one will believe them
- Wanting to forget about the abuse
- Fear of the unknown consequences of telling
- Not having the language to describe what happened to them
- Not understanding what happened to them until they became older
- Inner conflict generated by guilt about finding the experience pleasurable
- Fear of the abuser going to jail, leaving the family without a source of income

Some abuse is opportunistic, such as groping at a crowded event. These perpetrators hang around malls, arcades, parks, playgrounds, and beyond the fences of schoolyards. They follow children as they walk home from school and attempt to grab them when no adults are present. But most kids are groomed and lured into sexual abuse either through abuser contact with their parents or via the internet.

Knowing how abusers set up situations can help you watch out for potential abusers.

Victim Lures and Grooming

Some abusers befriend single parents by showing interest in the parent. Others show interest in the kids who seem lonely. They start with compliments and show sympathy for the parent who does not have the time or the resources to get the child involved in activities. They offer to babysit, take the kids to soccer games, coach the kids in a sport, or take them out for lunch.

Coaching and taking kids to games are similar to what Big Brother organizations offer kids from single-parent homes, but the organizations screen the adults who wish to participate.

Molesters who are family members use similar tactics with kids within the family. Some won't bother to be nice and use their size to make the kids engage with them. They arrange to be in a small space where the kids can't get away, like the kid's bedroom or a car, and overpower them. They are careful to pick kids who won't tell or will not be believed.

Molesters volunteer at events and activities involving children, where they select their victims and show special interest in them. Lonely kids fall for this attention because they want to be loved and admired. Their parents want to see the kids happy and appreciate getting help to care for them.

Some child molesters befriend unwitting kids on social media channels or online gaming platforms. Grooming begins with flattery. It then progresses to talking the kids into sending nude photos of themselves and ends with attempts to arrange secret dates.

Your kid may disappear one day. You don't know if they ran away or if someone lured them. Are they with the person who lured them? Are they still alive? Are they the victim of human trafficking? You don't know what happened to them.

Most recently, some enterprising criminals who are primarily interested in money have used similar tactics to talk kids into sending nude photos of themselves. Once they have the images, they threaten to release the pictures to their friends and family if they don't send them money. Sometimes blackmail leads to child suicide because the kids don't have access to money and are too ashamed to tell their parents.

What are molesters like?

Molester Profile

Molesters have the following characteristics:

- Both males and females molest kids.

- Molesters pick their victims carefully.

- Some, but not all, have been victims of molestation.

- When they're perpetrating the abuse, they think only of themselves.

- Many are married or in adult relationships in which they have access to children.

- They don't see the children as people but as objects to be used, like pieces of furniture.

- Somewhere in their lifetime, sexual arousal was triggered by children, which now continues as an obsession or sexual addiction.

- They find the sense of danger of being discovered exciting. Some commit the acts in the next room while the other adults are busy.

- When child molesters are not engaging in abuse, they typically fantasize about molesting kids. There are many outlets for child sex abuse material on the internet's dark web. The dark web is the part of the internet where criminals sell illegal goods and services.

- Molesters readily agree to tag-team parenting "to save money." When one parent or caretaker is at home, the other is at work, and vice versa. The schedule ensures access to the children and keeps them from dealing with a relationship with the other adult.

You Can Protect Your Children!

Protect your children. Don't let them become a statistic.

Talk with them. Work on improving your relationship with your children. Pay more attention to the difficult ones. They are the ones at risk.

If you have trouble talking to your kids, share stories about your childhood. Those stories can become a bridge between you. Be more patient and present. Keep trying.

You are the person between your children and real danger.

You are your children's champion, teacher, and protector. You care about their safety and their future. Worrying is a waste of time. Knowledge is power.

Conclusion

We've covered a lot of ground. Maybe you found that you already knew many of the things I've written about. Perhaps you tried some of the suggestions. Many examples won't apply to your children now, but they may in the future. Children are resourceful and ever-changing as they try new behaviors and techniques to get what they want. Information and awareness are your armor. Knowledge is power.

Attention is a recurring theme in the book. Children depend on our attention to meet their needs and to learn what behaviors will produce a positive reaction. As parents, we must attend to our interactions with our kids to avoid negative patterns and the formation of bad habits.

Understanding what is happening will help you manage the various challenges you may face with your children. You've learned the importance of patterns of thought and behavior in creating habits and interactions. You understand how to use modeling, shaping, and rewards to mold new behaviors and habits and extinguish unwanted behaviors.

Behavior charts have fans and detractors. You'll find them helpful in focusing your children's attention on behaviors you want to see more of. Your children will enjoy working for rewards and seeing their progress on the charts. If you have a controlling child, you'll enjoy the ease of sidestepping conflict as your child cooperates because of the rewards.

Parents and children have their own personalities. I tried to illustrate different ways of handling situations, from conversations to story telling to behavior charts to consequence lists. One or two of them might suit you best. Do what feels natural and what works with your child.

The most complex and frequent issues that brought parents and their children to my practice, such as morning routines, nighttime routines, bedtime battles, homework wars, manipulation, and debating, are complicated. They are also important milestones for kids' development into self-sufficient adults. As you work with your children on those issues, you'll develop a feel for their personality style. Understanding what is going on will help you handle other situations as they crop up.

There's a transition period from childhood to the teenage years. This is when your child seeks to separate from you and make their way among their peers. They are vulnerable at that age and need your love and guidance, although they pretend they don't. It's a confusing and emotional time for the parents and the child. You'll see glimpses of what they will be like as an adult.

The last section of this book tackles some heavy issues and possible mental health problems. I did not mean to scare you. Your child may not have to deal with any of that. They are in the book in case a parent needs that information and guidance.

Are you trying to do everything "right" as a parent? Relax. What is right changes over time. You are the perfect parent if you are kind, attentive, forgiving, and open to questions and discussion. If you shout at your child and say horrible things that you didn't mean, apologize and tell your child that you love them. It'll be a lesson in apologizing for mistakes we make.

This book was written to empower you as a parent and give you the knowledge and the tools to effectively guide your child's development and behavior with minimal effort and conflict. The goal is to have cheerful, resilient, confident children in a loving and harmonious family.

I hope you find a balance, worry less about what you're "supposed to do," and do what you can without destroying your peace of mind.

This book covers a wide age range. Keep it around for reference as your children mature and present you with new challenges.

Parenting is usually joyful, full of surprises and endearing moments. But when the fun stops, revisit this book.

This book is the first in the Your Journey to Successful Parenting series. I'm currently writing the other books:

- *Your Journey to Successful Parenting: Teens*
- *Your Journey to Successful Parenting: Autism and Hyperactivity*

Acknowledgments

I'm thankful to all the parents who read the rough chapters of this book as it was taking shape and offered advice on what was missing. I'm also profoundly grateful to my daughter, Elizabeth, who provided wise counsel on enhancements, improvements, and edits. Christine Grail, my editor, was meticulous and attentive in her corrections and comments. The illustrator, Karen Donnelly, did a wonderful job representing the instructions to clarify my recommendations. A special thanks to the team at 100 Covers who handled the cover design and to Jess LaGreca of Mayfly for her masterful job of formatting and publishing. She made the last leg of the publishing journey so much easier.

References and Resources

Braaten, Ellen, and Brian Willoughby. *Bright Kids Who Can't Keep Up: Help Your Child Overcome Slow Processing Speed and Succeed in a Fast-Paced World.* Guilford Press, 2014.

Díaz-Rivera, Mariano N., Agustina Birba, Sol Fittipaldi, et al. "Multidimensional Inhibitory Signatures of Sentential Negation in Behavioral Variant Frontotemporal Dementia." *Cerebral Cortex* 33, no. 2 (January 2023): 403–20. https://doi.org/10.1093/cercor/bhac074.

Douglas, Jessica, and Jan Scott. "A Systematic Review of Gender-Specific Rates of Uni-Polar and Bipolar Disorders in Community Studies of Pre-Pubertal Children." *Bipolar Disorder* 16, no. 1 (February 2014): 5–15. https://doi.org/10.1111/bdi.12155.

Faber, Joanna, and Julie King. *How to Talk So Little Kids Will Listen: A Survival Guide for Life with Children Ages 2–7.* Scribner, 2017.

Garey, Juliann, Laura Kirmayer, and Catherine Steiner-Adair. "Parenting Tweens: What You Should Know." Child Mind Institute. Accessed November 14, 2024. https://childmind.org/article/what-parents-should-know-about-tweens.

Selph, Shelley S., and Marian S. McDonagh. "Depression in Children and Adolescents: Evaluation and Treatment." *American Family*

Physician 100, no. 10 (2019): 609–17. https://www.aafp.org/pubs/afp/issues/2019/1115/p609.html.

Son, Sung E., and Jeffrey T. Kirchner. "Depression in Children and Adolescents." *American Family Physician* 62, no. 10 (2000): 2297–308. https://www.aafp.org/pubs/afp/issues/2000/1115/p2297.html.

Index

About the Author

Dr. Rogers has more than thirty years of experience as a clinical psychologist specializing in child and family psychology. Her expertise spans neuropsychological testing, therapy, educational consulting, and school-based interventions. Currently, Dr. Rogers dedicates her time to authoring books and articles on mental health and sharing her insights on Medium.com and on her website https://arogersbooks.com.

www.ingramcontent.com/pod-product-compliance
Lightning Source LLC
Chambersburg PA
CBHW071721120626
46550CB00001B/330